MICHAEL BURGE is an Australian author and journalist who lives at Deepwater on Ngarrabul Country in the New England region of NSW with his husband and their dogs.

His debut novel *Tank Water* and its sequel *Dirt Trap* (MidnightSun Publishing) are a rural noir storytelling cycle exploring homophobia and queer justice in the bush. A gothic mystery *The Watchnight* (Histria Fiction) is a bold re-imagining of the Methodist settlers who colonised Australia's Jenolan Caves in the 1850s. A memoir *Questionable Deeds: Making a stand for equal love* (High Country Books) lifted the lid on familial and institutional homophobia in Australia during the marriage equality campaign.

Michael has written, edited, directed and broadcast for Guardian Australia, Fairfax Media, United News & Media and *The Journal of Australian Studies*. A graduate of Australia's National Institute of Dramatic Art, he is a board member of BAD Sydney Crime Writers Festival and a member of the Australian Crime Writers Association.

His complete works can be found at www.burgewords.com

'I love reading Michael's work. An elegant, flowing pleasure combining journalistic rigour with literary excellence.'
                                        Margo Kingston, journalist and author

'It's time to move beyond a city perspective on rural gay Australians – so often imbued with pity, condescension and silly stereotypes – to hear our own voices on our own terms. Michael Burge is one of our most compelling, nuanced and enjoyable voices.'
                                        Rodney Croome AM, LGBTIQA+ equality advocate

TITLES BY MICHAEL BURGE

Fiction

Dirt Trap

The Watchnight

Tank Water

Closet His Closet Hers

Non-fiction

Questionable Deeds: Making a stand for equal love

Pluck: Exploits of the single-minded

Write, Regardless! A no-nonsense guide to plotting, packaging & promoting your book

Creating Waves: Critical takes on culture and politics

Plays

Merely Players

*For information about upcoming titles go to
www.burgewords.com*

QUESTIONABLE DEEDS

Making a stand for equal love

MICHAEL BURGE

Foreword by

SHELLEY ARGENT

First published in Australia in 2015 by www.burgewords.com
Reprinted 2019

This new edition published in Australia 2021 by High Country Books
An imprint of The Makers Shed www.themakersshed.org
Reprinted 2025

Copyright © Michael Burge 2015

The moral right of the author has been asserted.

All rights reserved. No part of this book may be reproduced or transmitted by any person or entity in any form or by any means, electronic or mechanical, including photocopying, recording or by any information storage or retrieval system, without prior permission in writing from the publisher.

Some names and identifying details have been changed to protect the privacy of individuals.

ISBN: 9780645270518

A catalogue record for this book is available from the National Library of Australia

To Jono and Richard

FOREWORD

2015

UNFORTUNATELY, THIS STORY is not a work of fiction. What happened to Michael when his partner Jono died still happens to same-sex couples in Australia, even as this book goes to print.

Lack of understanding, denial of relationships, and homophobic beliefs within families are just a few reasons the exclusion of partners still regularly occurs during an emergency or as the result of a death, and exposing these issues is one of the great outcomes of the publication of this book.

LGBTIQA+ equality cannot be properly considered without acknowledging that when same-sex couples are allowed to marry, the disenfranchisement of a grieving partner will rarely occur as routinely as it did for Michael.

A marriage certificate represents different things to different people. For some, it's the symbolism, the respect for the relationship or the inclusion in each partners' family unit. For others, it provides emotional, financial and legal security.

For Michael and Jono, a marriage certificate would have instantly proven they were legally recognised spouses and therefore next-of-kin to one another. It would have made the family dispute Michael has written about legally irrelevant, and lessened his trauma and heartbreak after the loss of his beloved life partner.

For society, a marriage certificate remains a very strong benchmark for relationship recognition.

While LGBTIQA+ couples are blocked from accessing Australia's Marriage Act, the recognition of their relationships, including de-facto family units, will remain at risk, particularly — as Michael's book illustrates — where death certification is concerned.

The rigid actions described in *Questionable Deeds* show there is still a long way to go in tackling homophobic attitudes and beliefs, but they provide more reasons to allow equal access to the legal protection that a marriage certificate provides.

As a parent of two sons — one straight, one gay — I could not imagine being cruel to the people my sons love.

As a family, we have embraced our gay son and his partner. We have made great friends and are part of a group that celebrates difference instead of fearing it.

My husband and I have always strived to encourage our gay son to be proud and live honestly. We would never want to deny his relationship in times of difficulty.

Same-sex couples have the same dreams, expectations and plans for the future as other couples, regardless of race and religion, and these need to be recognised.

I hope those who read this book see the need to speak up about how marriage equality is no threat to families, will not trivialise the institution of marriage, and cannot impact on Christian values or endanger society in any way.

What marriage equality will do is give same-sex couples the protections, choices and privileges that so many heterosexual couples take for granted.

Many see a marriage certificate as 'just a piece of paper', but realistically it's a protection for the rights and a guide for the responsibilities between all couples.

All couples should be given the choice to nurture a marriage, to learn by direct experience what that form of coupling means, and understand that only the parties to a marriage contract can decide its parameters.

2021

BY 2017, the Liberal-National Coalition was becoming more frantic when its right-wing members – of which there were many – could see support for marriage equality gaining momentum in the polling.

In desperation, after questionable campaigns inflicted on the public by right-wing religious groups, the government under Prime Minister Malcolm Turnbull engaged the Australian Bureau of Statistics to hold a voluntary national survey, giving Australians two months to respond. Fortunately, people did, and were overwhelmingly in favour of marriage equality.

After years of delays, a free vote on marriage finally came to Canberra. I sat in parliament every day of the preliminaries, often the only person in the gallery. However, on December 7, 2017, it was standing room only, and the air was electric in the gallery and on the floor of the House of Representatives.

When the vote was finally won, tears flowed, there were lots of hugs and people sang. But I was crying because the battle wasn't over. We knew the religious right had been promised a 'religious freedom bill' should they lose, and it was only a matter of time before it appeared.

In 2020, I decided it was time for me to retire from PFLAG and make space for a younger person with new ideas and more energy. I believe my successor Jane Hopkins has been the ideal choice for the role of National Spokesperson.

Now, in 2021, the discriminatory 'religious freedom bill' is looming large under Prime Minister Scott Morrison's leadership. The proposed legislation isn't about freedom; it's about religious privilege and cannot be good for any individual in a country that has been regarded as secular for some time.

I would like to thank Michael for asking me to write and update the foreword for his book. To me, it's not only an honour to be asked, but as an activist for **LGBTIQA+** rights — including marriage equality — it is such a privilege to speak out on what is a very important topic to me.

Shelley Argent OAM
(Former) National Spokesperson PFLAG
Parents and Friends of Lesbians and Gays

Preface

BEFORE I EXPLAIN my experience of loss, I need to explain my experience of gain.

Jono was my place of solace. We'd been moving towards one another for years.

Our meeting took both of us coming out of hiding. I came home to the Blue Mountains from England and came out to the community I'd grown up in, no longer afraid to deliver such news to my already knocked-about family, survivors of death and divorce.

Jono had spent years in the Bellingen Valley, licking his wounds away from the vagaries of big city show-business and the pain of a broken relationship, until he found the strength to follow a friend to the very same mountains. There, in the fold of one particularly cold winter on the cusp of the millennium, we found one another.

'Are you interested in me?' he asked me by the fireside of the only local bar we ever liked, 'because I'm besotted with you.'

At last, the perfect antidote to fifteen years of torturously hiding the truth, to the intolerance of any whiff of 'poofy' behaviour at my school, and the way the other boys seemed to work out I was gay long before I did.

My time playing it straight in a relationship with a woman, and my gay 'teenage' dalliances, delayed until I was in my very late twenties, all dissipated under the gaze of the first man who, thankfully, brought all that experimentation to an end.

We took our time moving in together. He was ready when I wasn't. By the time I was, he wasn't.

So we waited until it just happened in its own time, when it was the most natural thing in the world to live as a family.

A year later, we felt ready to relocate to the sprawling city of Sydney, the green shoots of renewed career ambitions coming bravely to our surface.

Neither of us was up to the fast-paced inner suburbs, but the spacious coastal suburbs south of the airport held a sense of permanent holiday that was the perfect way to fool ourselves, and we leased a 1940s house in Kogarah Bay on the strength of its retro feel and high fences to keep the dogs safe.

We assumed being only seventeen kilometres from the city meant our Sydney friends would visit us more than they had in all the years we'd lived in Katoomba, one hundred kilometres inland, and we laughed about all their excuses for not driving the short, scenic trip around Botany Bay to our housewarming.

Jono's old showbiz friend Amanda joked that if you lived south of Moore Park, you may as well be living in Melbourne. People are fickle. We laughed at that too.

But we talked seriously about moving our family again.

One Saturday, we met my sister Jennifer at a café and inspected a few rentals in Balmain. My side of the family, including Jen and our cousin Diane, had lived there for twenty-five years. Life in an inner-western suburb seemed preferable and affordable for me and Jono.

Jen was pleased at the prospect of us being near neighbours. We hadn't lived in the same suburb since our childhood home was packed up in the wake of our mother's death many years before.

'Don't you have a one-year lease?' Jen asked, the three of us sitting in the autumn sun.

I said: 'Yes, we do, but we can get out of it,' but I don't know why I felt the need to add: 'If someone died, they'd have to let you out of the lease.'

A few days later, Jono arrived home from his new job at a Hornsby bead bar. I'd been to collect the dresser we'd bought at a local op shop and filled it with our finest 1950s crockery in the dining room with a seven-piece pink, black and grey Fifties lounge suite. It was all looking fabulous.

Jono, being a dancer, twirled with delight as he encountered the scene, and said: 'Let's just stay.'

I was relieved. I hate moving, and the bright, inspired look in Jono's eyes was so priceless I knew we didn't need to go anywhere. City friends could get stuffed, our family was already home.

Too often, same-sex attracted people are asked to make a convincing case for marriage equality. To me, this is akin to explaining why the Earth revolves around the sun — you can say why you believe this to be the truth, using astronomy and physics, but that would not be good enough for some.

Saying that I found love with a man called Jono, that we lived together, ran a business, travelled, fought, made love, reared dogs, attended family events and shared our lives together, is not good enough for some.

So I don't try. The Earth revolves around the sun, and many people of the same gender love one another as deeply as people of the opposite gender. We always have. We always will. Case closed.

About six months after we started our relationship, Jono held me as I cried, possibly for an hour, my face turned away from him in shame, my sobs silent in shock and incomprehension at how hard my journey to him had been. That was the deepest love I'd felt since losing Mum.

We were not linked by anything as predictable as genetics, we chose to be with one another. We were life partners for over fourteen-hundred days. That's over fourteen-hundred reasons to be together, to stay by one another's side. That's enough to have our relationship enshrined in any law.

The day Jono twirled before our Fifties sideboard and said: 'Let's just stay,' we were embarking on a new chapter of our lives together, for better and for worse.

ONE

WE WOKE UP in my bed, both facing the window. Outside, the sun was already hitting the house across the road, and the old rose bushes in the garden showed in stark silhouette against the bright patches of light.

Jono was in my arms. We always slept in one another's arms.

We maintained separate bedrooms in all our homes — it just started that way, I don't remember why. Jono's was across the hallway, the same room used by the elderly couple who'd lived here before us, with its enormous built-in wardrobe; whereas ever since our relationship started, we'd negotiated nightly which of two beds we'd share.

He was due for work at Hornsby, on the opposite side of Sydney to our suburb, Kogarah Bay. It was a long drive, but he wasn't reluctant to do it.

We let the dogs in, made breakfast, showered and got ready. I was due to finish finding props and costumes for Jono's latest show — *Double Identity* — which was to open in two weeks at the Clarendon Theatre in Katoomba.

Before he left, I went into Jono's room. He was sitting on the white bedspread, the reflected light shining brilliantly through the pale curtains and onto his face. He took me into his arms — me standing and him sitting — and said: 'Thanks for clearing my space for me Mikey.'

The day before, while he was rewriting the show with co-writer Amanda, I'd tidied his room for him, sweeping away the dog hair and smoothing out his bedclothes.

We kissed, and soon after he was gone into the bright Sydney day. The last day of autumn.

I HAD plenty to do up in nearby Hurstville. Jono was working full-time at his day job and every other moment was taken up with preparations for the show.

I was running our household and assisting in the production and design of this important, professional engagement for Jono. Life was busy.

On the way to the shops, I spotted a green 1970s velvet modular lounge on someone's nature-strip. I made a mental note about where. When Jono got home we'd go and have a look. If it was still there, we'd probably take it home for the garage we'd just cleared to use as a his jewellery studio. The dogs would need something warm to snuggle into when the winter came.

I bought eight metres of dark green silk from a fabric emporium to make one of the show curtains.

I went to the magic shop on Rocky Point Road to buy some other show stuff. Against one wall were bins of every kind of glitter you could imagine. Every colour, every shape. I decided to take Jono there at the weekend, because he would love the bright abundance — and the slight ridiculousness — of such a shop.

On the radio, Gina Riley was being interviewed as Kimmy ahead of the new season of *Kath & Kim*. When asked why another series had been commissioned, Kimmy said she knew why such a hornbag like her was still on television: 'It's not rocket surgery, you know.' I'd have to tell Jono that one, since we often spoke like Kath and Kim around the house.

After the magic shop, I had to find my way around the back streets of Kogarah Bay, and came across a Girl Guides' hall, where hundreds of black, red and turquoise Fifties chairs were being thrown away.

So far, the retro-shaped chairs I needed to complete the set of the show had eluded me at op shops. It's always hard to find matching second-hand chairs, but here they were, free. *Jono will be pleased about that*, I thought as I rescued a few of them from the pile.

The day advanced with long stretches of low sun, the kind when the light always gets in your eyes because it stays close to the horizon.

I walked the dogs — Olive and Tully — down to the sports fields by the bay.

Both were young, fit Border Collies who loved to chase the low-swooping swallows that seemed to taunt the girls into chasing them, faster than any sheep could ever go. They ran home ahead of me, panting.

I'd taken over the corner of the large timber-floored room at the back of the house for the production's wardrobe department. The cast had been at the house two days before for a run-through of the show and costume fittings, so I needed to spend time working on various adjustments.

At around five-thirty the phone rang. It was Nathan, the male lead from the show. He was sick and needed to let Jono know he couldn't make it to the rehearsal that evening in Surry Hills.

I said I'd try to call the studio for him, and not to worry. I reminded Nathan how good I thought the run-through had been on Saturday.

Both he and the female lead Inês were young and keen and courageously giving of their time for an independent show. Jono and I always expressed our gratitude to them for taking part in something that provided them with no income for the time and energy spent. I did not want Nathan to stress about getting in touch with Jono.

I called the studio desk but got an engaged tone. Neither of us had mobile phones. It didn't seem in any way necessary to have them, so it was a stroke of luck when the phone rang again at about six. It was Jono.

He was tired from the long day in Hornsby. I told him Nathan couldn't make it, and suggested he come home early, but he said he and Inês could just go over some dance moves together, and they'd call it a night. I told him I'd found great stuff for the show. We chatted and laughed. I said I'd make dinner, and we said goodbye.

I started making pizza as the light of day disappeared. I had ABC television tuned to some history program by six-thirty. I can't remember what it was that day, but as I pulled my pizza out of the oven — I remember it had strips of green capsicum on it — I was so engrossed in the program that when the phone rang, I just let the answering service take the call.

Five minutes later I went into the office and checked the messages.

Amanda's voice, panicked and not making sense. Jono had collapsed and she was going into the rehearsal rooms. An ambulance had been called. Instinctively, I deleted the message and dug out Inês' mobile number.

She answered immediately, drawing great breaths. I asked what was up? She said they'd started first aid and had managed to get Jono back for a moment, but they were still trying to revive him.

I grabbed the keys, put the dogs out, made sure the oven was off, and started the car. The low fuel light went on.

As I backed out of the driveway I accepted that Jono and I would need to make some big life changes. If he'd had a heart attack at the age of forty-four, we would just adjust our lives around it.

Delayed in traffic near the airport, I imagined when I arrived he'd be leaning against the wall, looking a little worse for wear, while the ambulance crew packed its equipment away. I'd brush the hair off Jono's forehead and help him home. He'd been working too hard, after all.

As the traffic cleared and I took the usual route into Surry Hills, a deeper feeling came over me, one which had no visuals attached to it. I needed to get there to see all this fuss for myself. No amount of phone messages or mobile calls was going to give me what I needed. I needed to see Jono.

As I pulled up at the front of the studios, I mounted the kerb with my four-wheel drive and launched myself through the front doors.

Inside, the receptionist was dealing with a group of girls waiting for something — parents, probably. The scene was so very normal. No one was panicking. For a few moments I thought that meant nothing was wrong.

I said something to the receptionist. She pointed me up a flight of stairs, at the top of which I saw a team of paramedics descending.

In the middle was Jono, his face concealed by a mask, his upper body exposed by a shirt ripped aside. The crew let out a group sigh as they placed the gurney on the floor and immediately started pumping his chest.

It was so alien, so invasive of his personal space, that the desperation of the situation was immediately communicated to me.

Inês walked up to me, a moth fluttering, and said: 'There is still hope.'

Jono seemed to be stabilised, and they moved the gurney forward again, all of them registering in a heartbeat who I was to this man they were trying to save.

I instinctively stepped forward, but something beeped and they put the gurney down again, the disappointment clear on their faces. He was stubbornly refusing to come to life, so they worked on him some more, his body like a doll under their sudden, drumming attack.

There were other people coming in and out of doors. One of them, a mother, revealed she was a doctor, and she said: 'Right now, his heart is going like this ...' and she put her hands together at the fingertips and pumped them, like a spider doing push-ups on a mirror.

She disappeared as they carried Jono past me and down the stairs. Someone handed me his bag and personal things.

There was an ambulance at the door all of a sudden, and this lifesaving crew disappeared into it with Jono.

I followed, but missed which of the two ambulances he was in, having decided there must be two ambulances, because the one in front of my car, the one just leaving, didn't have its siren on. The other one with Jono in it must have rushed off into the night, the other way.

I'd been told the ambulances were from Royal Prince Alfred Hospital. I knew RPA, it wasn't far. I stuck behind the ambulance through a city that was coming home from work.

If he was in this ambulance, it wasn't racing because they must have stabilised Jono by now, and they didn't want to endanger the thousands of pedestrians who were getting in the way of us getting to the hospital.

At Missenden Road, the ambulance turned into the hospital precinct. I kept going to find a car park down a side street.

When I was out of the car I started to run, my entire body jolting with each large bound. Something about the night silence of the suburb was frightening me into this dash, across the brightly lit street and into the emergency department.

Amanda was there already, sitting in the yellow light within a deep fur coat. The receptionist asked us through into another room, where a male nurse joined us.

'You know that your partner's heart has stopped?' he asked me in a careful tone.

I said: 'Yes', waiting for the next part about them rushing Jono into surgery.

'Well,' the nurse said, 'we've been unable to start it again.'

My hand went to my face, but it hit me on an angle. I didn't care, I thought I was slipping off my chair. People seemed to be rearranged in their seats by unseen forces as I left the nurse and Amanda.

I was led into a corridor, where I watched how another nurse pushed a red button to open opaque glass double doors.

Behind that, in a curtained space, Jono was lying still on a gurney under a sheet.

It is true what they say about the newly dead appearing to sleep. Jono's face was relaxed, his skin pliable, as I brushed my hand across his forehead, the sobs starting to run through me like tremors. I felt the silkiness of his eyelashes as I kissed him.

Not yet believing, I opened one of his hazel eyes, and the gaping darkness of his dilated pupil met my gaze; a sudden wall against the life here, the emergency department of a Sydney hospital, and wherever he now was.

My glance must have been like a scan, both forensic and feeling. He was just so beautiful, a perfect version of himself, with his body's tendency to slump slightly sideways, chin dropping to his left shoulder, the way he'd always done in life in moments of vulnerability and cheekiness.

But the worst thing of all had happened to him, the very worst. The eyes told me that.

The green sheets around his naked body concealed all trauma, apart from the point at the top right of his chest where an intravenous main line had been inserted in an attempt to save him, and two small grazes on his nose and cheek where he'd knocked himself as he'd fallen to the floor, alone, in the rehearsal room.

But all that knowledge was to come. In that precious, solo moment I took in the reality of Jono's death.

'I will cry for you for a very, very long time,' I said, my loneliness coming back at speed.

Acceptance did not take long. Resistance to it is useless. I read years later how, faced with this moment, Yoko Ono had repeatedly smashed her head against the tiles of the hospital wall.

For me, the moment was filled with the memory of the grief of losing my mother at a young age, although I had the cold sense of how very much worse this was going to be.

I instinctively ran my hands over Jono's arms, his belly, and cupped his penis in one hand through the sheet, bidding those intimacies farewell.

After not very long, I tried to return to the hallway through the automated doors, but I found myself trapped in the corridor.

The exit to the waiting room was one way into the life to come.

Jono, and our life together, was in the other direction. When I chose to go back to him, a passing nurse came across me in my indecisive confusion, and pushed the button for me.

I went back to him for a moment. I don't know why. To see if it was true? It was. I don't remember anything about the next moment of separation, the walking back outside.

I sat down in a new room, and a young man, a counsellor, introduced himself to me. I needed to make some calls. I tried my sister Jen. There was no answer.

Amanda stood and hugged me, told me how sorry she was. For a moment, sitting in my chair, I was suspended in the naphthalene scent of her coat.

Somehow I was made aware that Amanda was going in to see Jono, but I made no objection.

I was in shock. The reality of Jono's death was being transmitted across the city.

The room was about to fill with strangers that it would take me hours to free myself of.

It never occurred to me that nobody in that place, apart from a medical practitioner, or me – Jono's partner and senior next-of-kin – had the right to view his body. His naked body.

Because I was unaware that my relationship with Jono was not ours alone. I had no idea in those precious, vulnerable moments that he and I were well and truly owned.

TWO

I MUST HAVE called Jen over twenty times on her mobile number, but it just rang out. There was a phone in the small room that had been allocated to me, and a few plastic chairs. The counsellor came and went, showing people I didn't know into the room.

One woman crowded my personal space, creeping right over any barriers I might have put in the way, looked me in the eye, filled my face with hers, and hugged me through a woollen poncho.

'What's happened to you, happened to me,' she whispered, gripping and unwelcome.

I was polite, I listened to her pain, but I completely disassociated myself from it. As soon as I could, I told the counsellor that there was no one in that room I felt comfortable with, and stayed in the corridor, expecting he would ask these strangers to give me some space.

I am not sure if he said anything, but they stayed.

I needed to keep calling my sister, so I went back into the room, trying to clear my way to the chair by the phone. It was like being in a doctor's waiting room — there was a common reason to be there, but no personal connection.

A familiar face came in the form of Inês, who arrived with her mother and a pair of police officers.

That seemed to clear the room a little, as they sat, offered their condolences, and started asking me and Inês questions about what happened.

She courageously recounted how she and Jono had joined the

back of a dance class in the next room at the rehearsal studios, doing *Moulin Rouge*-style dance moves.

When they returned to their own studio, he suggested they take a break, saying that his heart was racing.

Minutes later, when Inês returned, Jono was motionless on the floor.

Teachers were called. They started first aid. At some stage they seemed to get him back, but he didn't stay.

The police told me they'd need to take Jono's body to the Glebe Mortuary later that night, and asked me if there was anyone I'd like them to contact. I said no, I'd be okay to contact people. They said I'd be asked my permission about an autopsy, which would probably be performed the next day, if I said yes.

I tried to call Jen again. No answer, so I called my best friend, Claudia.

She answered almost immediately. My voice slid out of me with a traumatic note, as I told her Jono had died. She said: 'What?' with an almost complete loss of breath. I told her where I was, that I couldn't get hold of my sister. She agreed to come, even though she was two hours away.

The news began coursing through our community, at speed.

I thought to mention organ donation to the counsellor. He said they didn't do it in cases such as Jono's. I didn't ask why, part of me didn't dare.

Eventually, I got hold of Jen. It was the same as telling Claudia, the news slipped out of me on an unwilling breath. I left the room and stood by the door until I saw the welcome sight of my sister pulling up in the hospital grounds and running across to me.

I had to explain, and it was with sobs. She led me in to see Jono again. He was still in that soft state. My tears were really coming now, and Jen did something so sweet — she brushed them from my eyes and wiped them onto Jono's, trying to bridge that gap between us and Jono's oblivion.

We left him again, because now that we knew, we needed to tell Jono's mother and brother, half a day's drive away in Bellingen.

Jono's father Joe had died just six weeks earlier. Jono and I travelled up to Bellingen for the funeral. It was the last time his brother, Warren, and his mother, Maureen, had seen Jono.

This death was going to be more bad news for them, but I had a problem with delivering bad news.

So I rang Warren, who answered the phone as directly as I would to someone calling after dinner time. I could imagine the shock that must have registered on his face when I heard his wife Jane's stifled shriek in the background. I told Warren what I knew. He agreed to contact his mother. I gave him the number of the phone I was calling from.

Minutes later, she called. I wept openly now that contact had been made and apologised for not being able to call. She talked me through that, and I told her all I knew, that they were asking for my permission to perform an autopsy. I said it was up to us.

I said it was up to us.

All through those crucial, pain-filled minutes, I used the terms 'us' and 'we'. In my most panic-stricken state, I was inclusive without thinking. I shared without hesitation.

Everyone thought an autopsy was a good idea. We all wanted to know how a healthy forty-four-year-old man could suddenly die.

There was one more call to make, and it was also going to be a difficult one — to Jono's best friend Lisa, who was living and studying in Canberra.

Jen rang. After the news had been imparted, I was able to get on the phone.

Speaking on the fact of death in those moments, as both minds are assimilating, is neither easy or memorable, and I recall the conversation being thin and factual.

Lisa said she would come. She wasn't sure how or when, but she would come.

A nurse came into the room with a plastic bag full of Jono's clothes. I could not leave him to the cold night alone with nothing of his own with him, so I asked them to leave the small Buddha talisman he wore around his neck, and I agreed to follow Jen to her flat in Balmain.

Shock began settling on me. Outwardly, I displayed a greater than average normality — the ability to park cars and ascend flights of stairs — but inwardly the walls were collapsing.

I sat on Jen's sofa, and I remember it felt like the edge of an abyss.

Claudia arrived and we all started seeking solutions. The first question was where I would spend the night.

The dogs were at home. I wanted to go home. There was an offer from my cousin Diane, around the corner from Jen's place, but I talked her out of that.

I was on a desperate chase to find the closest scent of Jono, and that was at home.

We got into three cars and drove across the city. The fuel light in mine meant a stop at a service station in St. Peters, where I stood in the bleak light and carried out the most ordinary of tasks.

At home, I gave Jono's pizza to the dogs, who ran around in their usual state of welcome. Our voices were normal and our arrival held nothing special — Claudia and Jen were familiar to them.

We sat in the lounge room and slipped into a disbelieving conversation. Claudia and I had spent years as single flatmates talking over the unimaginable and the shocking in our family lives. Jen and I had spent even longer doing the same. Death was pitifully familiar to us all.

Eventually, I crept into his bed as though Jono was just late coming home from rehearsal.

I AWOKE to a moment of confusion, wondering where he was, before the reality kicked in and I started to sob almost immediately. Claudia came to my side.

I just didn't want to do the whole death thing, all over again. I said it out loud. Telling people, dealing with a funeral and all the planning it involves; but most of all it was the telling, and the realisation that nothing was ever going to be the same again. More than everything would change in multiple lives.

I even fantasised about telling no one and just saying Jono had gone away somewhere on a whim, but when the Coroner's office rang, seeking final permission to go ahead with an autopsy, all pretending was over.

I'd run my decision by Jono's mother and brother, and we were in agreement. We needed to know what happened.

The entire morning was punctuated by the ringing of the phone. Jen and Claudia answered it in stints, as we tried our best to let people know about Jono.

Some reactions included disbelieving laughter. One person assumed he'd killed himself. On and on it went, the terrible job of informants, shooting through lives like a bullet off course, and me feeling like I'd pulled the trigger.

The big question hung in the air, of course — what had happened to a youngish man who had everything to live for? I said we were still waiting to find out.

I retrieved the plastic bag of Jono's last clothes from my car. The plaid shirt we'd snapped up at a Brisbane op shop two months before had pinkish blood stains down its front; and his jeans, the well-cut second-hand pair in black denim, thirty-eight-inch waist, had been slashed by emergency scissors up the side of each leg, making them into bloodied cowboy's chaps.

He was so proud of those jeans, after being initially ashamed of wearing a larger size than he was used to as a younger man; but he looked so good in them I tried my best to allay his fears. Who, that loved him, was going to quibble about the waist size of a man in his forties who was finally growing into himself?

I threw them all into the bin. I didn't know where else to put such spoiled, precious things.

Friends arrived. People cooked, negotiating the small kitchen, stirring pots on the stove, keeping busy; or they sat next to me as I talked to others on the phone. I was held, hugged and supported, but the numbness was already settling in.

Eventually, a call came from the Coroner. They'd found no cause of death, toxicology on tissue samples would now be undertaken, which could take months.

What?

My reaction to that was matched only by my disbelief that Jono was dead.

A reason hadn't really been on my scale of priorities, but now that there wasn't one, the whole thing seemed unreal.

A call from Jono's brother Warren confirmed he and Maureen would be flying to Sydney that morning. We'd meet at the Glebe Mortuary, but I told him we had a mystery on our hands.

THE first day of winter was crowned by another stunning blue sky, which I noticed before we went into the darkness of the mortuary, and waited.

Maureen, Warren and Jane arrived. As lost souls together, we hugged and kissed, before the counsellors asked us in. There, under dark sheets, was Jono's body.

I placed a heart-shaped chunk of amethyst — the stone which is thought to aid the transition into death — onto his chest. Nothing about him was pliable. I walked quickly away from his frozen state.

I wanted to give the others space with their dead son and brother, so I stayed in the waiting room. The grief-filled murmurings of Maureen, starting to process, filled the silence.

Warren said they'd find a motel. He also muttered: 'They don't waste time, do they?' referring to the speed of the autopsy. I said we'd see them back at the house.

Into our home they came, seeking him, through every room, like a strange tour. Our bedrooms, our office, and Jono's jewellery workshop in the garage.

Then out came the photo albums, and the most surprising claim — that perhaps Jono could come back to life, even now.

'There have been cases of it happening,' Maureen said. I nodded. I'd heard about them too.

All I could think of was how little chance you'd have of coming alive again if you'd had all your major organs removed and weighed, and your chest cavity cut open for forensic inspection, because your partner had agreed to an autopsy.

Maureen was in shock, of course, so I decided to reach out and help her. I recalled what I'd already said to many that morning — how if anyone was going to skip out of their life the instant they'd seen anything beyond our existence, it was Jono. I knew he would have followed any light like a moth, no hesitation.

Warren's wife Jane showed a sense of love and respect for the Jono of that moment, eschewing photos (the past) for a quiet meditation by Jono's work table (the present), away from all the talk.

She silently searched his semi-precious stones, tracing the way he'd arranged them, and his tools, as gently as an archaeologist would.

That second night, my friend Judy broke through my numbness and put me to sleep by offering the simplified, basic cocoon of few facts and blanket comfort, and I escaped into it completely.

THREE

TWENTY-FOUR HOURS LATER, we all gathered at home to meet with the funeral director, Luke, representing one of Australia's oldest and most respected funeral companies.

The scene was quiet and caring. Claudia had collected her son Sam and was seated with him at the other end of the room, distracting him with a DVD. Around the Fifties table at the other end of the room were me, Luke, Warren, Jane and Maureen.

I was acutely aware of Maureen's experience of the same moment when Joe, Jono's father, had died only weeks before. Maureen and Joe had been separated for two decades, but lived not far from one another in Bellingen.

Jono had told me of her hurt when she felt the funeral director had not looked at her enough during their negotiations, so I made sure Maureen felt included by turning the decisions out to the rest of the people gathered at the table.

We all agreed on a secular funeral, with Jono's body to be cremated, no argument.

But I had an undeniable problem rising in me. I felt a physical connection to Jono's body that I simply could not put into words. All I knew was that I needed to bring him home before we took him to the crematorium.

Not wanting to have this whole issue extrapolated in front of a two-year-old sitting metres from me, or distastefully raising the issue of the funeral costs — which were my business — I simply said to Luke: 'I would like to bring Jono home first.'

Luke replied that this would mean Jono's body, by law, had to be embalmed.

I agreed to this procedure. Before I had to part from him, I wanted my man home. I had not caught up with the reality of it all yet, and I needed to hit the rewind button, to have that goodbye moment within our familiar nest.

I knew innately that if I could not have that, Jono's funeral was going to get ugly, and my grief was going to get even uglier.

Someone — I don't remember who — mentioned the extra cost of embalming. Perhaps it was Warren, fresh from the experience of his father's funeral bill? Or perhaps it was Luke, gently outlining what he needed to at that time?

In order to resolve the matter, I said I would be paying for whatever was needed to bring my partner home.

Then, we turned to the issue of the death certificate.

Sensing we were almost through the hard part of proceedings, I was also aware it was something that needed to be done just right.

Twelve years prior, I'd led a similar conversation at the funeral home where my mother's death certificate was created. At one end of the table, my grandmother struggled with untruths that had been rendered on her Germanic surname by a war, and fears about recording her beautiful Maori middle name.

So we'd assimilated the lies that would have been heartless to correct — onto an official document — considering the loss of her only daughter to cancer that morning.

At the other end of the table, my older brother Andrew and my younger sister Jen had sat either side of me, the three of us surrendering to the gentle but slightly officious questions about Mum's life.

Her marriage, long since ended, needed to be recorded as such to reflect her choices, and the details of the sibling who came between me and Jen, whose death at only two months of age had wrought so much quiet damage on our family.

So, when Luke suggested we create two death certificates for Jono — one for me, and one for his mother — a solution had been found before we'd even expressed a problem.

There was no response from the group about that decision, so I signed the funeral contract which had been sitting in a folder in front of me the whole time, and Luke and I moved to Jono's room, where the only thing for us to sit on was Jono's bed, an intimate place, while I picked clothes for him to wear in his coffin.

Shuddering as I did it, I chose pieces I thought Jono would be happy with, some jewellery and more crystals. Luke was very respectful of these moments. I farewelled him feeling that all was as well as it could be.

My cousin Diane had asked everyone to her home in Balmain for dinner that night, including Maureen, Warren and Jane, but they retreated to their motel. We all understood. Meeting new people in an acute state of grief was just too hard.

LISA was arriving into Sydney from Canberra by train, and on the way to dinner Jen and I picked her up at the Countrylink platform at Central railway station.

In disbelief, we wrapped one another in hugs, Jono's best and most constant friend, and his partner. Sydney's winter was already throwing cold breezes through the suburban night, so we bundled one another into the car and Jen drove us to Balmain with the dogs.

Dinner was the first social occasion I had to get through after Jono's death. I cried, but not for too long. Jono was just noticeably absent. Diane offered to put together some flowers for the funeral, and eventually we set out for the lonely drive back down to Kogarah Bay.

At home, Lisa did what everyone had done up to that point — she came inside and looked for Jono.

When she didn't find him, she curled herself up into a ball on the fabulous Fifties lounge and howled. We held onto one another as I took her into his room.

Straight away, she spotted what I had missed — Jono's runes. Not long before, she'd made Jono a set of viking runes out of beach stones, hand marking each of them with the symbols.

On the far side of his bed, Jono had left the runes untouched on his bedside table, with one sitting by itself on a crystal cluster — that rune was Dagaz, the stone of radical transformation.

THE next morning, like a bad joke, another bright blue day dawned. The house was full of people again, and barely had we all gotten ourselves ready when Maureen, Warren and Jane arrived.

I was in the living room sorting through photo boxes, Jen and Lisa were busy in the galley kitchen, when Maureen sunk herself into one of the bean bags and announced she wanted to take Jono's body back to Bellingen.

Jen flinched and looked at me, clenching her hands into frustrated talons, Maureen's back to her. I raised a hand, signalling to my sister that I would handle this. I let Maureen settle into the bean bag, then looked her in the eye.

It was one of those important moments we are called on in life to address, to step up to the plate. I needed a convincing argument in order to ensure the plan that was in motion — a perfectly good plan — was not derailed, but there were opposing forces at work.

This woman's son had died, but he had not lived in Bellingen for five years. His life had been in Sydney, and before that in the Blue Mountains. With family, friends and colleagues scattered from Brisbane to Melbourne, a Sydney funeral made it easier for everyone.

And yet, in those ferociously fast moments, I could sympathise. This was Maureen's version of me needing to bring Jono home in order to say goodbye to him, and I knew her feelings on the matter must be heard and acknowledged.

So I offered her something, from the heart. A memorial service at Bellingen, for her son. We would bring his ashes there, and another ceremony could occur.

'He was worth two funerals,' I said, relinquishing control of Maureen's plan for the second of them.

She nodded and smiled, the tears coming with the possibility of honouring Jono on her home soil.

The mood in the house went from tense anticipation to some kind of acceptance, as tea was made and brunch offered, that endless catering which accompanies the death of loved ones.

Then came another session of going through Jono's photograph boxes, but this time I was a little more aware of what was being pored over.

One box contained some photos that it was not appropriate for everyone to see. Jono had worked extensively as a model in his twenties and thirties, and there were some shots from a professional photo shoot where he'd been mucking around after the job was done, with a slightly pervy edge, taken when the model is prepped and demobbed before and after the formal shoot. In one, he was posing for the camera with his pants around his knees, wearing nothing but a dancer's thong.

Another photo, deeper in the box, was a nude shot which looked like the kind of photo you'd take if you were putting yourself on a gay dating site. Jono's face was obliterated by the flash that was going off in the mirror he posed in front of, but for obvious reasons I was able to identify him because I was very familiar with his anatomy.

For the first time I felt the need for privacy and I subtly took away one of the photo boxes and stowed it in the wardrobe in Jono's room, under a shelf almost at floor level. As I shoved the box in, I felt something else in there, and pulled out a thick notebook.

The pages were filled with Jono's instantly recognisable handwriting, which leaned back towards the left of the page.

It was a journal.

Excitedly, I flicked through and landed on a page where he'd written the words: 'I loved to dance' and inked over it a few times, making the words stand out from all the others.

'I loved to turn and jump and understand steps. The music, the movement, the flowing through space, moving from one side of the room to the other. The connection to people and the personalities.'

I'd discovered a precious treasure, but by the time I'd taken it back to the living room, Warren and Maureen had moved to our office at the back of the house.

Warren announced he was seeking a will. I told him Jono didn't have one, but he said he wasn't sure.

Suddenly, Maureen had papers in her hands, things from our joint files. I could see straight away it was Jono's superannuation statements, and Maureen was relaxing back into my office chair.

'Oh, he's given it to me,' she said, the relief washing over her. Not wanting to burst her bubble, I didn't clarify that Jono had nominated both of us as beneficiaries of his superannuation death benefit. I just encouraged her to put the paperwork back where it was now that she had found what she wanted.

Warren mentioned bank accounts. I laid my hand on them, and showed them Jono's personal account, which had been empty until a few weeks before he died, but now contained fifteen-hundred dollars, a payment he'd received for a choreography job.

Then Maureen said something which shocked me to my toes: 'I'll be taking Tully with me, just for a bit of comfort.'

In barely veiled panic I turned away and muttered something about not splitting up two dogs who'd lived with one another for years. In a sense I was talking about me and Jono, but our dogs were a natural extension of us, our family. Taking Tully would not be happening.

For me, that was the end of discussions around custody of dogs and bank accounts and wills and superannuation. It was all my business.

Lisa grabbed some of Jono's large sheets of paper and made a list of jobs that needed to be arranged and organised. Perhaps she also hoped she could shift the negative energy in the office.

Maureen, Warren and Jane left. We agreed to see them again the following day to meet the funeral celebrant at our home and go through the funeral plan together. As they departed, a palpable heaviness lifted from my heart.

THAT night I slept in Jono's bed, reading his journal, discovering all the reasons he'd kept it secret — the traumas of school for a gay boy, the fear of coming out and the obstacle course of sexual encounters with older men.

Then, his years of ballet training, and graduating into the Australian Ballet Company, with which he'd toured the world. Jono had often spoken mysteriously about leaving before his contract was up, but here the facts were laid bare.

'I was third or fourth cast for *Onegin*. I felt overwhelmed by the lifts. They said I didn't want to do it, so I got taken out and put in the chorus of the third act. I felt really defeated in that year and all that energy I had gotten into was fading. I started feeling silly in tights. I didn't want to be there anymore.'

He wrote of being accepted into the Sydney Dance Company and embarking on singing and acting roles, and a trip to London where he first saw *Cats* and came home for the casting sessions of the Australian premiere. When he'd held out for a larger role than the one he was offered — as some advised — he'd missed out altogether.

But life had taken a thrilling turn when he got cast in Andrew Lloyd Webber's *Song and Dance*.

'They stood up at the end of the show and we had a hit. I

received compliments for the first time about my dancing.'

I laughed at his account of finding a home at the age of twenty-five: 'It was fun to decorate a place the way I wanted it. I could sing to my record player. It was the first time I had really lived by myself.'

Jono wrote with great honesty about his loves and liaisons, his triumphs and failures, and a great turning point in his career, when he auditioned for a key musical lead in the late 1980s.

'I sang at Her Majesties for the Americans. They conferred and told me to 'sell it' this time through. I didn't know what they meant, so I sang it again without really changing it that much. I felt self-conscious but sang well. I was later told I got the role, it's just that I *didn't want it*. I guess I didn't have the pizazz.

'I felt defeated, but I was in love. I said I'd rather have a relationship,' he wrote, and embarked on recording his first long-term partnership. When that ended, he was at such a loose end he followed his family to Bellingen.

Gradually, the names and places Jono wrote about became familiar to me, as he documented the year we met in the Blue Mountains. There I was, in the last three paragraphs before the journal ended, a new discovery whose part in Jono's life was left unrecorded save for his first impression.

I felt a wave of disappointment.

There might have been some sense of Jono talking to me, had he written about us.

But it was clear when he wrote the journal he'd been in the phase of our relationship when we'd started encouraging one another to pursue creative dreams, dreams which became realities. I'd lived all that with him.

Exhausted from hours of reading about a whole life laid bare, a life which had just ended, I went to sleep confused, inspired, grief-stricken and determined to get Jono home.

FRIDAY was the longest of days. I drove to Hurstville for a haircut, parking where we normally would near our favourite op shop. In the salon I came clean about the reality of my week. The hairdresser didn't miss a beat, just did her job without fuss, and wished me well for the next day.

Soon after lunchtime the funeral directors parked a hearse in our driveway and brought Jono inside. I sent the dogs out into the backyard so they didn't get in the way or onto the busy road.

Warren told me his mother didn't want to see Jono in his coffin, and I respected that wish. He'd looked terrible at the Glebe Mortuary, and I didn't imagine that after being embalmed he was looking like the man we all knew and loved.

I wasn't sure I really wanted to see him either, but with his coffin parked beside my bed, the last place we'd ever slept together, I took the lid off and saw his face. In an instant I knew in my heart that all fear of separating from Jono's earthly remains was gone.

His body was now just a carbon copy of the real man, wrapped under a terrible white satin shroud with a frilly edge, which I immediately tore away and threw in the outside rubbish bin.

I couldn't put the lid back on, I just closed my door and left him safely inside, as the sun-filled room imbued him with a last sense of our home.

The celebrant arrived and took a seat on the fabulous Fifties lounge. He was not a large man, but he dwarfed the armchair, sitting awkwardly with one leg over the other. I realised how times had changed, in that such retro chairs were not designed for lounging on but sitting up and taking tea, only we were not taking tea, we were planning a funeral.

Maureen, Warren and Jane arrived as Lisa was cueing samples of music for the service.

Because she'd known Jono for so long, I'd asked Amanda to say a few words about Jono, and hoped she'd make it to the house that afternoon to be part of the planning, but she rang and said she'd see us tomorrow. I ran the song choices by her, and she thought we'd gotten them spot on.

We went through the service, based loosely on the classic funeral running order, but filled with Jono's favourite music.

Weeks before, at a privately staged early version of the new musical *Dusty*, Jono had leaned across to me and whispered that Dusty Springfield's 'Goin' Back' was one of his favourites.

The bittersweet longing of the words seemed to fit perfectly with a man who'd died so young, but it was the lyric — 'So catch me if you can, I'm goin' back' (written by Carole King and Gerry Goffin) — which really spoke to me of someone who had given us all the slip despite being much loved.

Then came the riskier tracks. Lisa had listened to them all, checking that there was nothing inappropriate in Madonna's 'Crazy for You', 'Nothing Really Matters', and other songs you wouldn't normally associate with a funeral ceremony.

I inwardly chuckled at the idea of Madonna having to audition for Jono's mother, but she did that day. The combination of the music and lyrics gently set Maureen off crying again, and we all acknowledged enough was enough.

The celebrant said his goodbyes, and the photo boxes came out again, while I wandered uneasily from the front of the house to the back.

This was my home, and I had planned to have my friends around, with Jono's coffin in the living room, and in some way acknowledge what had happened, to get a stack of pizzas and reconnect.

Maureen, Warren and Jane were welcome to stay, but Maureen had made it clear she did not want to see Jono in his coffin at home.

So I explained to Warren they needed to surrender to what we were doing. He made a gentle announcement to his mother that it was time to go. I saw Maureen to the door, but as we were passing my bedroom I asked if she'd like to see Jono.

She didn't resist when I took her by the hand and gently guided her to the side of the coffin.

A coffin is a well-designed enclosure for a body. Until you're standing right next to it, the height of the sides is such that you can't see anything, so I stopped and let Maureen go.

She continued towards her son, and I watched as the deepest, tenderest side of her, mouth open in anticipation, saw him in his familiar clothes and his jewellery, and his crystals.

'We are going to bring him out. Stay with us, if you want to,' I whispered. But they did not. I understood, but I was also glad I had gently tested the boundary.

I LET the dogs inside. Olive, the eldest, who'd grown from a puppy in Jono's company, sleeping on his bed and playing endless stick fetching games with him, summed up the whole week by sitting on the enormous white flokati rug in the Fifties lounge and vomited up a pile of bright orange balls — kumquats — which she'd shredded from the tree in the back yard.

The bitter pile of expression was swept up into the rug and Jen dealt with it in the laundry. I realised that I'd had no time over the past few days to give to the puppies, who still responded to hearing Jono's name mentioned, and would rush to the door, expecting him to be arriving home.

I comforted them as best I could, welcomed Claudia, her partner Murray, and their little boy Sam, and saw them settled in the back room for this strangest of sleepovers.

Then we brought Jono out. He looked terrible, really, so we did something about it.

Flowers had been arriving at the house, and we took the bunches of tiger lilies and filled all the space in the casket with them, surrounding him with dramatic colour and life.

Lisa and I held up the dogs. Lisa had Tully in her arms, and her kind, white face blinked at her dead master in his repose. She looked around at us all, dropped to the floor, seemed to already know what had happened, and, even more amazingly, to accept it.

Olive was in my arms. When she saw Jono she bucked like a toddler having a tantrum, wanted to get out of there, the sight, and no doubt the smell, so terribly wrong. She ran from the room and didn't return until much later that night, when we observed her curled on the floor between the legs of the gurney, eyes glinting in the semi-darkness, in vigil.

There was still stuff to do, plans to execute for the service, but everyone waited for me to do something. How else does a group of thirty-somethings cope with sudden death?

I stood by Jono's coffin and tested how I felt. Claudia put some music on and came to my side. The coffin, on its gurney, took the focus from everything else. All I felt was numb. All the scene held was blinding, impenetrable shock.

I decided to forego any grief and just go for take-away pizza. Murray came with me. We chatted while we waited for ours, shaking our heads and inhaling the disbelief.

Midnight passed with me still working on my eulogy, and Lisa giving me gentle feedback that it offered nothing positive. I added a line, freaked out when I couldn't get access to the printer to make a hard copy of it, and realised that the others acquiesced because I was grief-stricken, which I hated.

We all retreated to our beds and waited for the day to arrive.

ONE of Jono's dancing friends said earlier that week that she'd been to funeral services at the Eastern Suburbs Crematorium on rainy days and that the place could be a bit depressing under those conditions, so I harboured a prayer for a continuation of the stunning winter sun we'd been treated to in our grief all week.

And so it was.

The bright chrome of the gurney glinted in the sun as Jono was taken through our front door. Me and Jen had a giggle to ourselves at the over-solemn demeanour of the funeral staff. Slow and deliberate in their compassion, they were like robots, stopping the traffic coming down the road as the hearse pulled away and we followed.

As the cortège swept along the Botany Bay foreshore, Lisa started to sing a sweet song and I sang along, watching the rear of the hearse ahead of us in the traffic.

At the crematorium, friends were already mingling outside. I ducked into the outside toilet and saw a friend from the Blue Mountains, who asked me, in a knee-jerk reaction, how I was.

My response was just as knee-jerk, when I said I was okay. What else do you say?

Inside, we were greeted by Luke from the funeral company, who had the same solemn robotics going on. We had flowers and crystals in our hands which we wanted to put on the coffin, but first we took the lid off and allowed people to see Jono.

This began a procession of sorts. I greeted arriving friends and walked with them up the aisle, expecting them to peel off into their pews and avoid Jono, but to my delight they wanted to see him.

Naumi and her kids, with our friend Sarah, all held my hands and walked with me right to his side. People were putting things in the coffin with him. Maureen thanked me for adding the flowers.

A group of Jono's friends from his days at the Australian Ballet arrived. Two in particular — Jo and Liz — stood at the edge of their friend's coffin and openly wept. It was so very courageous and it filled me with gratitude that they could forgive us.

It sounds strange to say 'forgive' in this context, but there is something innately embarrassing about telling the world about the death of a beloved person, then holding a vigil with his body. It calls on deep courage within all of us, and I was so thankful that people joined in these simple, heartfelt moments, taking ownership of their part in the funeral.

The time came to put the lid on and start proceedings. Lisa, Jen and I were armed with flowers and crystals, but Luke, solemn and pumped up, held his arms out to make us pause as he went through the motions. We had another quiet snigger at his overblown demeanour.

An old friend later described the delight Jono's funeral instilled in her, from the music to the eulogies, and the crystals we shared with everyone in his life.

We encouraged people to take one or two they felt drawn to from the display outside the chapel, made from the stall Jono and I had transported for years to various regional markets, and the dramatic bolt of deep green satin I'd purchased for the show on the day he died.

I listened to Jono's brother Warren speak of a boy they cherished, born in the wake of the loss of another brother who'd drowned as a child when the family was on holiday. Warren spoke of the shock, and regret, that Jono had died 'just when he'd started getting his life together,' and I felt like wincing. It was Warren's truth, sure, but it wasn't Jono's.

I listened to Jono's friend Amanda speak of a man the show-business industry had cherished, willingly accepting an Australian Ballet dropout into the commercial dance world.

Tellingly, Amanda asserted: 'And he was mine', before Claudia's little boy Sam, who was sketching on the floor before the lectern, wailed, which encouraged Amanda to add: 'And he was yours too ...' which made even less sense of her rather mysterious statement.

Then I got up to speak.

Since Jono had spoken to me, intimately, of his time as both a son and brother, of his feelings about being a 'replacement child', about the inner workings, both inspiring and corrupt, of the Australian show-business world, there was plenty I could have said.

But I wanted to focus on the real man.

I wanted to speak about the Jono who'd found himself, and shared that self with me, despite all the competing forces outside our relationship.

To do so, I had to publicly admit what he felt himself — that in show-business terms, he'd always been too delicate for the spotlight. He'd had to dance around it almost his whole life, but in the years I'd met him, he'd learnt to work in the performing arts without needing it, without paying the high cost for it, like some others in the room.

I also had to bridge a vast gap in order to express who Jono was: a bundle of calm spiritual energy, but also showbiz personified. He communicated through the languages of dance and movement, but also had higher messages to impart than those that got rounds of applause.

He was also my partner. My husband, ostensibly. We were everything to one another. I didn't expect or need anyone to understand. The public concepts of gay marriage were not the slogans they are now, but marriage was the only word to describe the relationship between Jono and me, so I used that term.

I also wanted to deliver a message of hope, a sense that this was not a life truncated, especially since that sense of regret had already been offered to the room. I wanted to imbue people with the idea that Jono had achieved so much of what he'd set out to do, that his work had been well and truly completed.

To achieve that, I asked the gathering to join together 'in the greatest standing ovation this venue has ever seen,' and they leapt to their feet in a wall of noise.

I walked forward into it, met Maureen across the aisle that divided us, took her hands in mine and lifted them in the spirit of love and belonging. Her creased face released and she drank it in; we both did, because even as it peaked, this life-enlarging energy began to slip though our fingers.

THE niggling pain I'd felt all that week reminded me that at some point I was going to have to leave Jono's physical remains at the crematorium and walk forwards into my life.

Secretly, I envisaged creating a bit of an involuntary scene at the side of his coffin.

Thankfully, I'd agreed with Maureen and Warren that we would have no 'closing of the curtain' moment, or allow Jono's coffin to be conveyed through the doors in the wall of the chapel.

People began to file out into the sun, seeking Jono's crystals, and the solace of company. I had no plan, I only needed a moment to say another farewell.

The coffin was closed and I didn't want some big scene of opening it again. I just walked up to the head of the box, put my hand on it, and trembled a little as I concentrated on that beautiful face I'd witnessed at the emergency room, minutes after Jono had died, when there was a sense of peace, escape, release and of transition.

With that in my mind, I released myself from his body, and turned away.

Jen was there waiting for me. I'd done the same for her at the funeral home where Mum's body was on view.

Mum died in her own bed at home, where we'd cared for her with the help of her nursing colleagues and friends. I'd wanted my last memory of her to be the still-pliant figure in familiar surroundings, but Jen had wanted one last look and bravely went in by herself.

Now, we were grief-bound siblings yet again, and the first people we encountered as we left Jono were our brother and father. Dad put an arm out to delay us, his long-estranged younger children, and muttered a few platitudes about calling if we needed him. Andrew seemed keen to get away.

My dear friend Sal was at the end of a pew slightly further back giving me that look of hers, an almost naughty acceptance of life's vagaries. It was priceless and comforting. Somewhere in that look I forgot Dad and Andrew, and walked into the sun surrounded by friends and loving sister, where the world did indeed feel as safe as it possibly could with Jono lying dead inside the chapel.

Some of Jono's cousins who I'd never met introduced themselves, including one who bore a striking resemblance to him, which was a nice surprise, since none of his immediate relatives looked in the least alike.

Friends chatted in circles, and some familiar faces emerged from the crowd, including friends from my graduation year at the National Institute of Dramatic Art (NIDA), and high school in the Blue Mountains.

Jono's friend Liz hosted a wake at her home in the Eastern Suburbs, where I spent the first hour talking to people who were trying to get away by offering their condolences and disappearing, and the second hour dealing with a very strange show-business acquaintance of Jono's who kept asking me inappropriate questions about our sex life. He didn't seem to know about the other wake at some pub for the showbiz crowd, insisting on knowing where everyone was.

Somehow my intention to stay for only a little while and get home for the dogs slipped through my fingers, and I got stuck with this overbearing retired dancer, take-away Chinese dinner which took ages to arrive, and my completely unfounded concern that our hosts might have wanted people to go.

Sometime quite late we said goodbye to Maureen, Warren, and Jane, who were leaving to return to Bellingen the next day, but said they would drop in at home to say goodbye. Jen drove me home to Kogarah Bay.

The funeral was over. There was nothing more to look forward to.

SUNDAY'S weather slips my mind, although it comes to me as a grey day, the kind of windswept conditions I would hate if I had to go to the airport and fly anywhere.

The house already had an empty feel to it, and I was reminded of the need to buy a heater sooner rather than later. Since moving from the Blue Mountains in the spring, Jono and I hadn't needed one.

Sometime in the stark morning, Maureen, Warren and Jane came by before they left for home. Of that meeting, I can recall only one thing — that Maureen wrote me a personal check for fifteen-hundred dollars.

I hadn't asked for it, but I didn't put up any barriers to receiving it.

Standing in the kitchen, away from his mother, Warren muttered to me: 'Maureen is going to take care of all of us, even you,' although I gently waved him off in an attempt to articulate I didn't need any taking care of.

I assured them I would collect Jono's ashes from the funeral company. Jen and I would bring them to Bellingen as soon as we could arrange it, in order to have another ceremony up there.

The week had come to an exhausted, pitiful end for which a grey day must have felt entirely appropriate. No need for the falseness of blue skies and bright reflections. I just felt flat, and I also remembered the rent was due the next day.

FOUR

THE DARKNESS WAS as deep as the abyss inside Jono's dead pupils, and felt every bit as watchful.

In the distance, a narrow river skirted along the back of nearby suburbs, where the hum of the city was rent by the periodic rush of planes landing and taking off.

The scrubby slash of sand lay silent between the main road and the bridge over the water. Cars of all kinds, parked hurriedly, showed the place where men had entered the bush, but there was no sign of anyone out on the road, where the lights of passing cars might point them out.

The wire fence meant entry through one of two gates. I parked at the head of the line and ducked into the deeper shadows quickly, a thick jacket insulating my rushing heart against the coastal breeze.

Narrow pathways revealed themselves. Tea-tree boughs brushed against the nylon of my parka, making more noise than I wanted. Silence, then planes, then silence again, but a city silence that only feels like silence, and my heart beating.

Nobody. Finally I admitted the cars might not have been there for the reason I thought they were. Perhaps it was just extra parking for commuters, more convenient than crossing the network of freeways that skirt the edge of the city?

Where the scrub came to an end, I turned and made my way back along the track. *I'll get in the car, just go home*, I thought.

Then a rabbit shot past my feet and took the right hand fork ahead of me, flitting into the grassy verge and away. Jono taught me that rabbits are a symbol of good fortune, so I took the right-hand pathway.

More coverage, darker and more dense where the great canopies of the tea-tree groves would serve as vast umbrellas for picnickers in the sunlight. At night they shielded the eyes of the world away, and well they might.

Figures manifested like shades, barely moving. The odd glow of cigarette ash. I felt prone, so I turned back, yet again, to see a figure looming behind me.

We passed. I noticed his strong scent. Keen eyes, like mine, showed underneath a cap. We both turned at the same time, and the dance began.

He led me into a side path away from the others and kissed me tenderly. He was caring. Soft. He didn't need to force me to my knees, I launched myself into his groin, which held the strongest part of his scent, and he released the day's cares onto the soil, then started on me.

He encouraged me on, like an actor, saying that if we'd been at home in bed we could have taken all night.

Then we came apart, each to his own shadows. I found my way back to the car and disappeared into the light, the satisfaction gone before it ever arrived.

SEX. One minute it was there for me, with Jono, all the monogamous, beautifully intimate sex we could ever have wanted. The next minute it was gone. Two double beds in the one house, and both of them empty.

A fortnight after his death, I found myself wandering into an upstairs sex shop in Rockdale, buying a latex penis and a pornographic DVD. At home, the penis seemed so out of place, unattached to anything. I tried to use it and I failed, dismally. It was all just so sad I ended up in waves of shame.

The DVD was full of alienating scenes. One attracted me, with its sham intimacy as opposed to energetic fucking, but it was still just fleeting sensations without any of the reality.

I threw both rubber penis and DVD away.

But the drive was still there. I imagined Jono while I masturbated, the way he'd press his face to mine while he was in the deepest pleasure, but the images never captured the man.

But the drive was still there, and so I traversed the beat near the river, feeling the shame that an unfaithful lover might.

It was a world I had very limited experience of. At the lonely end of every town, sometimes by a railway line; or the far end of a sports oval, there's a no man's land. Sometimes there's public toilets, but not always. Often, men seek out sex in the elemental surroundings instead of the stink of urinals.

Whether they use beats or not, all men generally know where they are. They form part of drunken carousing at the pub. *Saw you down by the railway line last week Davo*, we say to one another, ribbing, but one man in that conversation has the location of the local beat implanted in his consciousness, one curious man. He might have a wife and three kids, but eventually he'll find his way to the wrong side of the tracks for sex with men.

I once had a lover, Gary, who introduced me to beats, not long after I came out. I was incredibly naive and thought a picnic in the bush near the harbour meant a basket full of homemade sandwiches. Gary laughed, pointing out the men waiting in the scrub, and the others watching from the moored boats.

'This is what it's all about,' he said, exasperated, in an attempt to teach me. I packed up and left, torn between a sense of propriety and a sense of attraction. I liked Gary, but I did not want to make love with him in the open with anyone watching. All in a rush, I realised why it was I spent so much time waiting for him while he went to a public toilet on our days out.

As I climbed back up to the car, I passed a family, as oblivious as I'd been, about to enter the beat. Gary followed me, with two young men wanting a lift back to the city with us. I agreed and endured the innuendo between them all, realised in a shamefaced rush that this wasn't what I wanted. This man was not my lover. He wasn't even a friend.

This is not what it's all about, for me.

THE week after Jono died, a television show we'd anticipated was broadcast — Tony Kushner's *Angels in America*, a drama that ripped open the HIV-AIDS crisis. Judy asked me to watch it with her at nearby Bexley, so I fed the dogs and left them at home for a night.

With Judy gone early to work in the city, I lingered in her sunny flat. We'd painted it the year before, and in such comfortable surroundings I felt okay, until the dreadful realisation hit me that I had nothing to do.

Had Jono not died, that week would have been filled with more rehearsals for the show, days of constructing the sets and finalising the costumes.

I would have been flying to London a week after the show opened.

The momentum was still there, somehow, and we were all talking — me, Amanda, Inês and Nathan — about the show still going ahead, but deep down I had come to harbour another terrible secret, that I knew I simply couldn't do *Double Identity* anymore.

When I imagined it, I anticipated the terrible pain of wanting to call for Jono, with only others to answer, others who had no ability to comfort me the way he would, with his light touch. More than a limb was missing, yet there was no visible blood.

That morning, I toyed with the idea of just doing the show anyway, *Angels in America* and its dark warnings to all hypocrites a stark reminder in the light of day.

But when I got home I was simply unable to enter the room where all the costumes hung on a rack in the place where the only performance of the show had taken place.

The Clarendon Theatre needed a decision — Jono had booked an entire winter of weekend shows — and they would need to find a replacement if we cancelled.

I sat on my decision quietly. Towards the end of that week, I had an appointment at the funeral director's office to collect Jono's ashes and his death certificate.

It was an important step to take, because everything about Jono — his body, career, finances, life choices, hopes, energies, and his past — all had been transformed by fire, and the economy, into so much ash in a box, and this one very important document.

Luke was busy when I arrived, on the phone at the far side of a high reception desk, so I sat in the sunlight of the company foyer, all the accoutrements of the funeral industry at my disposal.

He emerged holding a large box and something else pressed to the top of it, wearing what at first impression was an awkward grin.

The box, enclosing the familiar grey plastic bottle of ashes, was heavy. Before I could really take its weight, Luke pressed the other object into my hand — a chocolate frog.

I let out a surprised laugh, and thanked him, then asked if I could have the death certificate.

He'd already started turning away, lifted a hand to wave me off, and said: 'Oh, you'll need to talk to Jono's mother about all that,' before retreating through the doorway of his office.

I blinked. He returned to shuffling papers at his desk, and I caught his eye as he checked to see if I was still there.

What Luke wanted, and what I gave him, was for me to be out of the office with Jono's ashes under my arm, and a chocolate frog, so he could acquit the funeral contract to the next stage.

JUDY took a morning off work and drove me to the rehearsal studios in Surry Hills early the next week so I could collect Jono's car.

We were greeted by the woman who'd been wearing the poncho at the emergency department, the one who'd lost her partner to sudden death a short time before.

She was quick to share with me that the business had named a rehearsal room after him, and showed me the plaque bearing his name, hanging above the door. In her mind, I could do the same for Jono.

I nodded, knowing that I would never go ahead with such a thing. This woman's partner had died while out in the bush jogging, and I assumed there was no plaque to mark the spot, in the same way that I did not want the slightly shoddy-looking dance studio where Jono died to bear a written memory of his death.

I said how fitting I thought her plaque was, but in my mind I just didn't want to join her 'plaque club' at that moment.

Then I met a choreographer, one of the teachers who gave first aid to Jono after he'd collapsed. I thanked her for trying, a rather obvious thing to say.

On the stairs where I'd witnessed the paramedics trying to revive Jono, I felt I was in the wrong area. The stairwell seemed too narrow, because I remembered a vast place, where space opened up between me and the unfolding events.

But it was just a blank-looking stairwell, now empty.

Upstairs, the room where Jono had danced at the back of a class gave onto another smaller room, where Jono had called for a break because his heart was racing. There, in the corner, he'd collapsed and hit his head on a chair.

It was really just a warehouse with peeling paint and high windows, like so many places where creativity is hatched, giving onto rooftops where pigeons busied themselves with fighting and roosting.

I'd had enough. I made a few pleasantries and excused myself.

In the dim light of the garage I saw the last traces of Jono's journey from his day job in Hornsby — his lunch wrapper discarded by the gearstick, a shopping bag in the back seat, with a red sweater he never wore. The receipt told me the time of the transaction — his last lunch hour.

WHILE walking the dogs at the local sports fields, I let them both off the leash under an enormous tree and they sped off after the swallows.

Before I'd passed back into the sunlight, a large clump of seeds fell right at my feet. One second earlier and it would have hit me on the head.

I looked up into the eyes of a large white cockatoo, hanging upside down with its wings spread, dangling and turning its head comically, swapping which eye was looking right into me.

The moment was surreal and brought Jono to mind.

Later, on the phone to Maureen, I related the incident, when she asked me how I was. She shared an experience she'd had that week, walking out of her hairdresser's in Bellingen, only to be confronted by an unkempt homeless man who addressed her directly and said: 'He's safe, where he is, your boy,' right out of the blue.

We let these memories settle between us, and eventually I asked Maureen if she'd received her copy of Jono's death certificate yet.

She said because we were waiting to find out Jono's cause of death, they hadn't been issued yet.

AMANDA rang me, full of banter about us doing Jono's last show together, then surprised me with a very strange question.

One of the other teachers at the rehearsal rooms had given Jono mouth-to-mouth resuscitation after he was found unconscious. There was blood from the cuts he'd received to his face as he fell and struck a chair, and Amanda was wondering, out of the blue, was Jono 'healthy?'

'You know, did he have that certain disease, *to do with blood?*' she coaxed.

In a rush I realised she was asking me if Jono was HIV positive. I muttered a few platitudes about how her friend had nothing to worry about. Amanda rang off quickly.

After more than two decades of HIV-AIDS carving its way through the show-business community, some still talked in euphemisms?

I CASHED the cheque Maureen gave me, because she said it was to cover Jono's share of the rent. It was very kind of her to think about things from that perspective, and the money would give me four more weeks of effectively sharing that house.

I cancelled my tickets to London and told my friends over there what had happened. Sympathetic, shocked emails came through.

But I couldn't get an immediate refund out of the travel insurance company. They said they could repay the bulk of the ticket costs when I sent Jono's death certificate to warrant his death and his relationship to me.

Claudia and Murray suggested I come and stay with them for a weekend, the weekend when Jono's new show would have opened at Katoomba, but also the three-day gay-friendly Queen's Birthday long weekend in the Blue Mountains, with a dance we would have gone to.

Naumi said she'd go to the dance with me, if I wanted to. I imagined the heaving mass of celebrating people, and decided there was no way I could front up to it without Jono, so I remained non-committal, just packed up the dogs and drove west for a break from Kogarah Bay.

Claudia and Murray had just moved into an enormous house Murray had created. Being a builder, this was his dream home right on the bush.

Things were still being finished off, but it was a great, solid piece of architecture, and the newness of it all, the thick stone tiles of the massive bathroom, the broad beams, the panoramic views, were blindingly distracting for me considering the state I was in.

I slept in a front room downstairs which was not carpeted and had no furniture. I didn't care, it was just great to be in another space, closer to the elemental bush, and despite there being no fence, everyone helped me keep an eye on the dogs.

We lost Olive at one point, sparking a slightly desperate search of the property, temptingly close to the bush for a curious dog, but she was found nestled in a pile of brown velvet curtains under the stairs, watching us walk past in our panic, our calls becoming more and more acute and preventing her from declaring her whereabouts in case she was in trouble.

Life just could not, should not, bring me more loss at that point.

Claudia's sister and her husband came to stay the same weekend, which was a little awkward for me because I did not want to impose my state of grief on anyone. So, in the afternoon, I decided I'd get out of their hair and go to the dance anyway.

The afternoon took too long to pass, as I read a book on my makeshift bed and avoided the family gathering as best I could. I felt angry at myself for coming that particular weekend, prone to meeting people I didn't know very well, worried about the dogs annoying their very small children.

So I took a walk, but couldn't access the bush anywhere — it was sealed behind private property in every direction. Tully chased a cat back into its driveway, and the owner screamed at me to put her on a leash. I screamed back that she should put her bird-killing cat on a leash too, and headed back to the house, defeated.

A pink sunset arrived and I got ready. Naumi came to collect me. We stood at the edge of the family dinner, and excused ourselves, giggling into the night like we always did on Blackheath Dance night.

In the frozen dark, people queued, waiting to pay their entry fee or smoking in clusters, the cold air making their exhalations ever showier.

People, mostly men, milled in and out of the Blackheath Town Hall, eyes darting to check out who was there.

I wasn't really in the mood, but I went through the motions, greeted the ticket sellers brightly, got my arm stamped at the door and bought my raffle tickets.

Inside, the dance floor was already full, men and some women grooving to the usual mix. Naumi and I headed for the stacks of chairs up the back where we always left our coats, scarves and hats, before diving into the crowd.

I suddenly felt vulnerable. This was the very worst place to come.

I recognised some faces, was looked over by others, and just felt reluctant about the whole damned thing.

JONO and I had met at this dance, exactly five years before.

In fact, we met in the car that a friend, Brad, was driving that night. I'd hopped into the front, and Jono was in the back. I couldn't see him, I could only hear him, and he sounded assured and gentle, not loud and mawkish, the way some people come across at a first meeting.

As we emerged from the car I saw his beauty. He noticed me looking, but we were part of a group that gossiped and pushed its way into the hall. It was my first time there, and Jono's, so we went with the flow.

Inside, we headed up the back. All the tables were full, reserved by the slightly older crowd who made a night of things with wine and food.

But I hadn't brought anything. Neither had Jono. Someone said there was a bottle shop at the pub just down the road, so we'd said we'd both go and buy some booze.

I led the way. As we pushed into the cold air, a set of knowing faces seemed to realise Jono and I were meant for one another, and were indeed going to get together, better than we did.

We walked in silence. I read in him the signs I was probably exhibiting, that fear of entering the male-dominated air of an Aussie pub, with its wall of testosterone.

Jono's eyes were wide, and, as I held the door for him, my chickening out allowed me to see him up close for the first time, the way he held his head, and the way he moved.

After that I don't remember much apart from stolen glances on the dance floor; moving to a ridiculous ABBA melody that went on and on; wondering if Jono was with Brad, the guy who'd dropped us there; and being descended on by Gary and Claudia, who'd caught the train.

Gary kept manhandling me, and I kept fending him off. We were over by then. I didn't deal well with his wandering eye and his constant engagement in sex in public places.

Claudia had brought the great news that one of our favourite bands — the Eurythmics — was recording again and had announced a world tour. There was a talent show, we all cheered for the queers and raised hell in the strait-laced town of Blackheath for one night, and Jono and I had met. There was great potential in that.

At the close of proceedings, Claudia and Gary bundled into Brad's car, lying across Jono in the back, and we drove home. Brad made sure to drop us off first, and, as Claudia and Gary and I got out at my house, where Claudia rented a room, Jono exclaimed: 'Oh do you all live here together? I'm so jealous!'

I made sure he knew it was just me and Claudia.

Brad looked put out, wanting to whisk his prize away. Gary came in and led me into my bed. I was drunk and high on hope, so I let him, but it was for the last time.

BY the time Jono and I had been together a few years, we'd regale that night, reminding one another what a web of lies we'd met in.

Jono thought Brad and I were together, and he set out to separate us. I thought Jono and another guy we collected on the way to the Blackheath Dance were lovers, a mistake that Brad was not keen to correct.

Now, five years on, Claudia surprised me and Naumi and arrived slightly after us, just like she'd done the first time we'd gone to the dance, the pain on her face an acknowledgement that this was a new era.

She'd put her kids to bed and come anyway, a generous act of acknowledgement that our ridiculous attendance at the dance that year needed numbers to make it work.

A few people recognised me, and acknowledged what had happened. Melissa asked me to dance, and our gyrating occurred while she told me her happy memories of working with Jono on a council project. Josh and Rodney had a quick, sympathetic word with me, before melding into one another's arms.

Only one person asked me where Jono was — Lavinia, the magnificent cross-dresser — as she walked to the stage to judge the talent show. I had to raise my voice over the music to give her the bad news. She froze, not one part of her glamorous visage took it in, and she sailed onwards, as though it just wasn't true.

FIVE

BACK IN SYDNEY the winter was settling in. I bought the heater Jono and I had planned to buy together. I walked the dogs. I went grocery shopping. I went to the swimming pool and did my laps. I watched television.

Gradually, the painful truth of living alone dawned on me.

Jen said she wished she had room for me to move in with her, but she lived in a tiny studio apartment. Judy also thought about taking me in, but two working dogs in a unit was just not going to work.

Claudia and Murray said I'd be welcome to live with them in their enormous home. It was a generous, welcome offer, but I declined.

I needed to stay, for some reason.

It felt as though Jono was just away. I'd believed my own wish that he was not dead at all, just on holiday. Sometimes I would mention his name to the dogs, and they'd launch themselves to the front hall, the way they always did when he'd arrive home from work.

Only now they'd stand, wagging tails dropping in disappointment. It was cruel of me, but I did it to maintain a kind of illusion for myself as much as for them.

One day I gathered all the flowers that had filled the house for over a fortnight, took them up the end of the backyard, shredded them into smaller clumps and threw them into the compost bin, a large black cylinder with a lid.

Stalks went in first, all the gerberas, daisies, roses and others.

Then handfuls of petals, in great layers that filled the enormous bin to the rim. Framed by the black plastic, the contents looked ridiculously bright. Living, thriving flowers were suspended for just a few days before they would rot and die, lose their volume and their colour, and return to earth. Beautiful, beautiful compost we had, the month Jono died.

THE week of Jono's death I was in that dreadful show-business state of unemployment. I was 'between jobs'.

The truth was I'd managed to get myself sacked from a production of *King Lear* at the Newtown Theatre a few weeks before, but I saw the break as an opportunity to use my design skills to complete the costumes and props for Jono's show *Double Identity*.

He'd been overjoyed about that turn of events. We were working together, again, just like we'd always done.

We had a great routine that made magic out of the broken career dreams in our wake, me and Jono. I'd had trouble finding work in Australia after my years in England and started producing my own films. Jono's extended hiatus from performing had led him to work on his own shows, but neither of us was making any headway in 'the industry'.

We loved to take long drives, and very quickly we worked out what great planning time a country spin provided. On one of our first, to the south coast of NSW, I'd ventured that he could just keep producing his own shows, nothing was stopping him. His journal told me what an important moment that was for him.

He encouraged me to develop my skills as a writer by keeping up the regular drafting of script ideas.

Gradually, we formulated a series of joint projects, including a film festival and a series of stage comedies, in addition to work we both started getting with other companies.

We got into the habit of never letting the other fall into despondency in the wake of each project, not because they weren't successful, but because show-business can feel very transient. Groups come together and work intensely for a short period, then people go their own way.

Jono and I would treat ourselves to a short holiday to distract us during the period when we were likely to feel down about the end of a project. Every time we drove home, the next phase of our collaboration would be hatched by talking it through.

So when I'd had enough, spoken my mind and was let go from *King Lear*, Jono just shrugged and suggested we move our holidays up a month — the long drive to Queensland would sort things out.

Between Sydney and Bellingen, we wrote an entire one-act play we planned to enter into a short play festival. We wrote the lines by speaking them in character and worked out the sets and costumes and lighting. We always kept it light and we always kept it fun.

Then came the opportunity to pitch a show to The Clarendon Theatre. We'd already produced one the year before for this great independent venue — *She Males from Outer Space!* — and had it picked up by the Sydney Gay and Lesbian Mardi Gras cultural festival for a season in Newtown.

Once the run of the new show — *Double Identity* — was underway, I was going to the United Kingdom for three weeks. My sacking from the cast of *King Lear* had inspired plenty of career soul searching, and I gradually formed a tentative plan to start writing freelance articles for extra income between rare acting work.

In England I was planning to try my hand at travel writing, and undertake some research for plays of my own, while Jono had his head down for six weekends of shows at Katoomba.

Our lives were taking off in all manner of new directions when he suddenly died.

Everyone said *Double Identity* should just go on without Jono, but I knew I couldn't do it. I kept getting mental pictures of myself stepping alone into the joint role we'd fulfilled for one another.

He had been seriously achieving in his last weeks, but there had been much anger welling up in him. He'd get off the phone after conversations in which production obstacles had been placed in his way and shook the desk while he groaned and complained.

That was the theatre producer emerging: frustrated, bold and assertive. I was learning to encourage him to keep things light.

He was striking deals with business people, attending meetings, making decisions, budgeting and executing his own choreography and acting work, and he was starting to cut ties with old collaborators who were noticing the change from submissive 'yes' man into theatre powerhouse.

I was happy to help, but to step in when he died? To work with some of the people he'd decided to work with?

No, I couldn't do it in my state of grief, yet the final decision seemed to rest with me.

I made a few emailed platitudes of 'thinking about things' while I was away for the weekend in the mountains, but when I got back to the city I quickly announced that I was not going to continue with the show, but the rest of them were welcome to do it. They could have access to the costumes, props, sets, tapes, and all the stuff Jono had planned, but I was not going to step into his shoes, not for his sake, and not for mine.

The silence, after my email about this decision, was deafening.

The first sound came from Warren, Jono's brother, who called and made a time to come to the house at the end of that week to collect Jono's car.

Jono's father Joe had given the little white Honda to Jono two years before, when he could no longer see well enough to drive. It was a generous action which replaced Jono's little old bomb that was barely holding together, even just getting around the small but hilly township of Katoomba.

We loved Joe's car. We went everywhere in it, on holidays, for work, with the dogs, with friends. It was a tiny vehicle, but we seemed able to transport theatre stuff of vast proportions in it.

I knew that legally it wasn't Jono's. I had a car of my own, and the same kind of energy that assisted in getting rid of the flowers helped me agree to giving Jono's car back to his brother and his mother.

They didn't need it, but they said they were going to keep it for family and friends visiting Bellingen, and that possibility included me and my sister Jen, since the plan was to take Jono's ashes up for another memorial ceremony.

Warren was catching a ride with a friend in a truck, transporting furniture to the city. He'd use Jono's car to drive home.

That week, Lisa came back from Canberra where she was in the middle of her busy design course, to help me deal with Jono's things.

We made light of Jono's fabulous collection of retro op shop clothes as we bagged everything up. None of it fit me apart from a few shirts and tops, which I gently housed in my wardrobe.

In his dirty clothes basket was an unwashed shirt, heavy with his scent, which I kept under my pillow.

Lisa got busy writing little notes which she secreted into jacket pockets and other places in his clothing, which would inform the new owner about the special man who'd once worn these items.

During this sheer, distracting fun, Warren rang from somewhere on the road. He sounded a little awkward, but I'd learned that was par for the course with him. He always seemed slightly uncomfortable in his own skin. He gave me a time. I said I'd be at the house to meet him.

All I was really worried about was Jono's dog Tully. I was determined that there was not going to be any discussion about her being taken from me and Olive. To make that point indelibly, Lisa agreed to take both dogs for a walk while Warren was at the house.

He arrived and asked me how I was. I told him I was okay, since I didn't know him enough to get into it.

Jono's ashes were sitting on our Fifties bar ready to go with Warren to Bellingen, for Maureen's sake. She'd also asked for a pair of his tap shoes, which I had ready, with a box of family photographs and other documents I felt they ought to have.

We chatted. It was stunted. Warren was like an alien to his own brother, so he was hardly going to gel with me. He remarked on how much weight I'd lost, barely a month since Jono's death. I brushed it off, having been oblivious to getting skinnier.

Without Maureen, her only surviving son seemed lost. I detected a little empathy for my situation, and he seemed slightly embarrassed at being sent to collect things from his dead brother's house.

But I helped him through the awkwardness by saying Jen and I would come up sometime, perhaps in the spring, although Maureen should just pick a date for Jono's memorial service in Bellingen and we would drop everything to be there and help.

He was gone after a short time. I cried at seeing the last of the little white car Jono and I had so many laughs in over the years.

THE next morning, Warren called from somewhere on the road not far from Sydney. He'd spoken with his mother overnight and she'd made him call back with a list of things she didn't want him to leave Sydney without.

These included the television and video player Maureen had purchased for Jono before we met, and many of his files and plays. It was a detailed list that was a sudden attack on my sensitive state, while being beguiled by Lisa's gentle world of fun around Jono's personal effects.

Jono and I had combined two households into one. We shared everything. Taking a television from the house meant taking my only television, not his. It was an inappropriate thing to be demanding of me at that critical stage.

I got off the phone. I needed help. I needed advice. Lisa kept bagging up Jono's things, while I called the Gay and Lesbian Legal Centre in Darlinghurst.

After hearing me out, an organised young woman asked me a

few pertinent questions about my relationship with Jono.

The crux was our rental agreement, signed, in both our names, and the complete lack of a will.

There was no doubt: everything in our home was now legally mine, and I had all the proof I needed to back up the claim. I thanked her and called Warren back, telling him, as gently as I could, that he had the car and the rest of the things I was happy to give them, but he could take nothing else.

Lisa and I did our best to get back into the fun zone so we could do the unthinkable: take Jono's clothes in bags to a clothing bin down in Kogarah Bay. We bundled it all into the car and made a little ceremony of the whole thing.

At home not long afterwards, I picked up the phone to check for messages.

There was one from Maureen, upset and grave.

'That information you found out about what you can and cannot inherit, that's *wrong*,' she said. 'Those are my son's things!' she asserted.

With a knee-jerk reaction, I deleted the message. I didn't want such angry words in my life.

The bubble had burst. Warren was possibly on his way. I suddenly didn't want to be there when he arrived. Lisa suggested we needed someone to negotiate on my behalf.

So I called Claudia, and she agreed to talk with Maureen to see if she could be mollified.

Lisa and I tried our best to distract ourselves with afternoon tea while we waited.

When Claudia called back, her voice was a little shocked.

Maureen, apparently, had a big list of items she required Warren to collect when he arrived. Claudia had tried to negotiate, but was met with a brick wall, at which Claudia had said: 'So, it sounds to me like you want everything?'

I was to also deliver up Jono's entire collection of crystals, which Maureen had already promised some friend of Jono's in Melbourne I'd never met or even heard of.

When Lisa revealed she needed to go back to Canberra that day, fear about Tully hit me like a wall.

Tully was registered in Jono's name, but she was ours. I was the one who'd taken care of her through all the nights Jono was busy choreographing and working. I was the one who talked Jono through the time Tully had been gravely injured and almost died. She was an integral part of my life. She was not going anywhere.

To add to the stress, it became clear there was a direct line of communication between Maureen and Amanda, when Amanda emailed about my decision on Jono's last play, saying that I was making decisions about something that was not mine to make decisions about.

The language was typical. Once, Amanda had been what's known in the industry as a 'gatekeeper' — someone to pay in some way to get ahead in the industry — and Jono had been her sidekick many years before. Now, with him gone, Amanda and I grated, like two bones without cartilage.

The feelings of powerlessness about Tully, about Jono's things and his show all came crowding at me in a rush. Knowing I'd be alone when Warren came, I made a plan.

I called Claudia and asked her to make a take-it-or-leave-it offer to Warren. He could come at nine-thirty the following morning and collect the entire set of costumes, props, sets and paperwork for Jono's final show, and they could produce it if they felt it was that important that 'the show must go on'. Everything would be on the front step, but I would not be there. Nor would the dogs.

I realised on some level that my time in our lovely holiday house near the sea was coming to a swift end, as I moved everything from the large dance studio at the back of the house to the front porch.

Early the next morning, I bundled our paperwork into the car with the dogs, bolted the gate, locked every door and window, and we went to the beautiful open sandy beaches of Kurnell.

By the time we'd returned there was nothing left on the front steps, not a trace of the production that Jono and I had sweated over. *Double Identity* was now entirely in their hands, and I no longer felt safe in my own home.

SIX

MY LEGAL STATUS was some comfort to me, now that I knew about it.

Late in 1999, the year Jono and I met at the Blackheath Dance, the NSW Government finally bowed to community pressure which had been applied ever since the peak of the HIV-AIDS crisis: to give some legal recognition to same-sex de-facto couples.

So many gay men had come out to their parents, then informed them of their imminent deaths. So many caring, bereaved, patient partners had watched their men die, many of them ailing themselves.

The issue of where these estates went — to the parents, or the surviving partners — caused an unknown level of disenfranchisement, much of it silent, now lost in the morass of decay and death that swept the international gay community in the 1980s and 1990s.

Jono and I were blissfully unaware of the reality of our relationship's legal status; ignorant, really.

Very early in our courting, I made a few hard-nosed references to gay politics, and Jono simply brushed them aside.

Such matters would not concern us. I acquiesced to his preference for freedom of thought, because I didn't really know what I was thinking or talking about.

Yet by the time our relationship was legally detectable, legislation was in place.

The Property (Relationships) Legislation Amendment Act was the earliest, enshrined into NSW law in 1999, and, by the time Jono and I were cohabiting in 2002, further amendments were added.

These were the protections that the staffer at the Gay and Lesbian Legal Centre had relied on to inform me of my rights.

The most important right the Act bestowed on same-sex de-facto spouses was next-of-kin status to one another. As such, we were from that time permitted to act on the other's behalf in certain legal matters and able to inherit, particularly in cases of intestacy.

One of the most important responsibilities it expected of us was to lovingly prepare for the worst, as far as death and incapacitation of one or both was concerned.

Rights. You never get them unconditionally. They always come with responsibility.

Jono had been sexually active from the late 1970s, the very dawn of the HIV-AIDS pandemic. In the early 1980s he toured internationally with the Australian Ballet's Dancers' Company, recorded in his journal as a whirlwind of performing, sexual opportunity and drugs in a world of experimentation.

Yet he'd always sought committed, monogamous relationships. Eventually, he found one, which lasted for a couple of years.

When Jono and I met, we revealed our HIV status to one another, another responsibility enshrined in law, granting the right of sexual expression.

Apart from his superannuation death benefit nomination, listing me and his mother, Jono left no indication of his legal wishes as far as his estate was concerned.

In the absence of him expressing his responsibility to me, the state of NSW bestowed responsibility on him the very moment we told our friends we'd met someone special, and were keeping some of our clothes in one another's homes, in September 2000.

I remember our glow reflected back to us in the faces of our friends, celebrating our 'honeymoon period' with those who'd hoped both of us would meet a man to make a life with.

It was a joyful, celebratory time, and we revelled in it, while we opened one another to a life of possibility.

It was a blessing that we didn't have to care about the law, and that we were required to ask no permission or fear legal recrimination.

Had we known how free we were, we might have celebrated much more and made our relationship's expression all the louder and clearer to those who might have feared the ramifications of two men who had found their soul mates, if only for the sake of all those who had suffered without the protections of the law.

When I recall those early years of same-sex equality, I realise now why no one was really celebrating, because the imminent danger for men sharing their whole lives with other men would remain for years to come.

LISA shared something with me which was a great help in my grief — she taught me to meditate.

It was a very simple process. I would sit in a relaxed state, focus on visualising a safe place in which I could communicate whatever I wanted to anyone by whatever means.

I tried it a few times and what I manifested was a place just like the set I'd designed for *Double Identity*, a below-street office in New York with the legs of people passing by slightly above in my peripheral vision.

An image of the prop phone I had found for the show was the means by which I imagined I was able to communicate.

In my first meditation, I reached out to Maureen and Warren. Things had been fraught between us, but I wanted them to know I bore them no ill will.

I enjoyed the escape and clarity of this calm dialogue, but after Warren's second trip to take things from our home, during my next meditation I was jolted as I visualised construction workers in overalls and hard hats.

A voice said something like: 'We're having problems,' and 'just stay out of the way,' and I saw that my safe place had collapsed.

Slick black slime was coursing down great chunks of concrete and there were emergency crews at work, shoring up the place from further collapse. It reminded me of scenes from the 9/11 attacks on New York.

I retreated. Lisa suggested I try again and make it safer, but I never did, it was too much of a shock to see that a black ooze was infiltrating my life within in addition to my life without.

So, I did the only thing I knew how to do, because I had done it before — I went back up the mountains and stayed with Claudia and Murray.

Claudia and I had known one another since we were kids and went to the same secondary school.

Our mothers had been friends. We shared plenty of history, including the eighteen months she'd lived at my home in Katoomba in our own version of *Will and Grace*, both single, both facing big issues. Mine was coming out. Hers was addiction. I went to a gay men's support group. She went to twelve-step meetings.

We encouraged one another through seminal moments of our young lives, including the weeks when Murray courted Claudia by arriving in his little blue builder's ute and taking her out for the afternoon.

Eventually, they moved in together.

The brittle, recovering woman I'd opened my home to without judgement had evolved into a lovable person, and despite the loneliness I felt without my friend, her departure inspired me to find a love of my own.

So it seemed the most natural thing in the world, not long after arriving at their enormous house on the bush, when Claudia approached me again about moving in with them.

Without thinking, I said yes. It seemed serendipitous. I desperately needed a non-judgmental place for me and the dogs.

'You can just mope about the house, exactly as you are,' Claudia said.

'Oh, I won't do that,' I said.

'Well, we won't care if you do,' she replied.

'Well, if you're sure ...' I said.

'Just pack your stuff, and come,' she repeated.

She and Murray left for work and I was feeling positive, so I decided to contact the funeral director and just get Jono's death certificate directly from him. After all, we'd agreed on it.

Luke was immediately evasive. 'You'll need to talk with Maureen about that,' he repeated as my questioning got firmer.

'But you remember, Luke, Jono was my partner,' I said, getting anxious.

'Well, that's not how they put it,' he replied, trying to settle me down.

'What?'

In that big, new house, the truth settled on me with a cold swipe on a sunny winter day. Something terrible, possibly irreversible, had taken place, the kind of aberration that set flocks of loud birds screeching through the bush to announce a disaster.

'What exactly did they say? Be careful Luke, this is very important,' I said.

'They bullied me into it,' he confessed, 'they said you were not partners.'

He was so upset about it I just let him go without challenge.

My first response was to find a way to fix the problem by telling whoever needed telling that Jono and I were partners, that he would want me to have his death certificate in my grief.

I toyed with calling Maureen directly and demanding she give it to me, but something stopped me, a combination of the visions I'd had in my meditation of that black ooze, coursing through my safe emotional space, and the deep anger and hurt which I might have unleashed on her in her grief.

I also felt innately that I should not have to ask anyone for what was my right.

THE sudden loneliness of living by myself was a motivating factor when I agreed to a visit from my old friend Christine once I was back home at Kogarah Bay.

We had not seen one another for almost three years before she'd kindly come to Jono's funeral and spent time talking with me at the wake.

There was no definite end to our friendship, which had begun at NIDA over a decade before, when our names were selected at random to have our student card photos taken in the same session.

Both nervous new arrivals — she in the acting course and me in the design — I was awestruck that this Pre-Raphaelite beauty would have anything to do with a deeply closeted boy from the sticks.

We were in the same orientation group, and eventually we moved into a shared house in Newtown with Christine's boyfriend Terry, an actor from her class.

The house was pink, and the arrangements replete with *Sophie's Choice* comparisons. Me, the awkward country virgin like Stingo, lived downstairs. Christine was the misunderstood siren Sophie, and Terry the troubled Nathan, were upstairs, all in our own version of Yetta Zimmerman's pink palace in Brooklyn.

We were every bit as doomed.

Terry got chucked out of NIDA like so many do at the end of the second year of the acting course. Another acting student moved in, and I just made it easy on all of them and moved out.

After NIDA finished, Mum died and I went overseas for six years, but I kept up my friendship with Christine. Something about my grief and my closeted state made me write to express my love for her, which she gently rejected.

Years later, after another relationship breakdown, Christine came to live in my house in Katoomba.

I'd come out in the interim, and Claudia was renting the front room after one of her stints in rehab.

The three of us spent hours sitting on the front verandah of the old mountains cottage, talking one another through break ups, sexual adventures and life's misfortunes, but when I called time on the bitching and encouraged Christine to take stock, to lift herself from misery and forge ahead, she disappeared.

By the time she reappeared, Jono and I were together. Something about our approaching cohabitation shone the light of clarity on my life. I'd had a glimpse of what it would be like to live as a family, to have the courage to reclaim familial life over sharing houses with flatmates.

I don't know if it was confusion or jealousy, or both, but that clarity wrought havoc on my friendship with Christine. Fatigued at being roped into her latest scheme to shoot an audition piece in our home, Jono expressed to me that he was not enjoying the process.

This was at the time when he was reclaiming his own life, and we'd spoken at great length about changing from the facilitation of others' creativity to nurturing our own.

He was right. There, in our kitchen, working on take after take of Christine's showreel, which would never succeed in getting her an audition for a film that had, no doubt, already been cast, I realised I was up to my ears in her creative needs.

Ever since that first moment in her glow, I'd been willing to foster her creativity. I was like a slave to it. I championed it. I anticipated having a part in it. It was doomed territory for a real friendship.

In the best way I knew how, I expressed my transition to Christine, and she disappeared, again.

The next time I saw her was sitting at the end of the pew in the chapel at the Eastern Suburbs Crematorium, respectfully present. Afterwards, I told her of my acting adventures, small fry compared to her amazing achievements on screen and stage.

So, when she rang and offered to visit me at Kogarah Bay, some of the glow was still there.

When she crossed the road from the railway station and got into the car, we hugged and I cried, apologising that Jono was not there to meet her too, because I felt bad that her disappearance had meant she never got to see him again.

We went to see a play at Sydney Theatre Company, revived our common sense of humour at the absurd display of theatricality on the stage by snorting through an entire ridiculous sequence, and mingled in the über-cool theatre scene in the bar after the show.

Head spinning from the changes wrought on the family life that had flowered with Jono, and accepting with great sorrow that all fantasies of finding a conventional life with a woman or with a man had eluded me, I dropped Christine home and drove around the bay under a sparkling Sydney sky, straight back to the beat near the river.

I FIND moving house painful and I avoid it wherever possible.

Jono and I had spent plenty of time packing and unpacking — we'd moved four times in the years we were together.

There is nothing like the process of moving to test the limits of a relationship. Jono sprained his ankle on two of the moves I'd helped him with, and spent time with his feet up while I did most of the heavy lifting, but we laughed through most of it.

When we eventually moved in together, I made a nest for him in the Katoomba house I'd lived in for four years, while he took a short trip to Bellingen, an annual winter event for him.

I was happy to repaint the two front rooms for him in colours that he chose. One he used as an office from which he produced his shows. The other was his bedroom — we agreed we'd each have a bedroom to ourselves, although we shared a bed every night.

While away for that week in winter, Jono made a flippant mention on the phone about having to see a doctor because he'd had heart palpitations. Knowing how stressful he found the trips back into the awkward fold of his parent's separation, I understood feelings would have been heightened for him.

But heart palpitations? That was something else.

Not long after we moved in together, while we were watching television, I hugged him from behind and felt the steady beat of his heart. For a moment it reminded me of what the doctor said, but his heart rate seemed so regular, so calm. We were living together as a family, we'd saved another dog and two ducks from the pound. Life was good, we were thriving, there could be nothing to worry about.

Now, faced with moving yet again after such a brief nine-month stint in the city, I just couldn't muster the energy to go through with it, so I asked my sister Jen for help.

I knew that I needed to be able to drive away one morning with the dogs and not see our whole lives taken apart, so we settled on a huge garage sale, with a few pieces of furniture going into a truck bound for the Blue Mountains.

I would meet it at Claudia and Murray's place and unpack a room's worth of my things there.

When the day came I departed swiftly, as though it really wasn't happening. I had my focus on something else.

On the way, I attended the read through of a play I'd been cast in — Harold Pinter's *The Dumb Waiter* — at the Q Theatre in Penrith.

The director, Sherreen, had gone out on a limb and asked me to consider the role of Gus, one of two hitmen holed up in a basement awaiting word on their next job. It was a courageous offer considering the timing, but I leaped at the chance to have something concrete to do.

The read through went really well. It was exciting to inhabit the role of Gus, and I dived into the part with a rough cockney accent inspired by Eric Idle of Monty Python.

Me and another actor — Andrew — would be performing the first in a double bill of Pinter's one-act plays, with two very experienced actors following in *The Lover*.

A new house and a new job, just for a while, just enough time for me to sort out where I would go from there.

It had been sunny in Penrith for the read, but, as is so often the case, by the time I arrived in the Blue Mountains it was raining.

At Claudia and Murray's place, the truck had arrived and most of the unpacking was done, but I walked into the first moment of angst during my stay in their new house.

It was the pathway of drop sheets, a bit of mud trodden into them in the unpacking process, which rang a prescient bell through all of us. Claudia and Murray seemed to have already had 'words' about that before I arrived.

I took matters into my own hands and saw to it that every last trace of mud was removed from the sheets and the new floor.

The house was Murray's dream home, a heritage-inspired symphony of recycled timber, capacious in the extreme, with many places for its residents to find privacy.

Jono and I had joined the celebration picnic the day they'd purchased the block, and visited the build as it progressed. I'd also supported Claudia in having her say about some kind of office space for her in the design.

Although being the architect and the builder meant Murray chopped and changed as he went along, there were a variety of rooms Claudia would be able to find her space in when they moved in.

Murray had been kind enough to push through the carpeting of the downstairs bedrooms just in time for my arrival, and within an hour I had everything I needed set up and ready, and it was thankfully really comfortable.

The dogs were a bit of an issue.

There was no fence to keep them in, but there was a huge deck which I could house them on when I was not home. I felt the weight of responsibility about them, shifted around by circumstances as we were, but both dogs got on well with everyone.

That first night we all just started getting used to one another — me, Claudia, Murray, and their kids Bill and Sam. I went to bed early to give the family some space. I was already noticing how fatigue was catching up with me very quickly.

The next day, the sun returned and I felt more at home, a feeling I decided to enhance by going on an enormous grocery shopping spree for the household.

While preparing for that, I got a phone call out of the blue.

I'd known Nadia for over a decade by then — she was the solicitor who'd helped my mother win a maintenance case for due alimony for Jen's tertiary education. That was in the last year of Mum's life and she'd been trying to ensure her youngest was well looked after by her ex-husband, financially if nothing else.

Nadia had acted as one of Mum's executors, and so when it came time for me to buy and sell my first house, the house Jono and I eventually shared before we left for the city, I'd asked Nadia to oversee the conveyancing. I knew and trusted her already, and she was happy to do the work, during which she'd met Jono.

When she rang, Nadia had just heard he was dead. It's difficult to ensure everyone hears about a death, but Nadia waved off my apology about that, asked if I was alright, and said: 'You'd better come in and see me, are you in the mountains?'

'I can come in today, what's the rush?' I asked.

'Well, I heard about Jono from a solicitor in Bellingen in a phone call. There's a transcript of the conversation. It's odd, because Jono's mother and brother are claiming they did not know he was in a relationship with you, and they're saying they didn't know he was gay until he'd died.'

I drove immediately to Nadia's office and while I waited, she peered around the waiting room doorway and gave me an update: 'They're now saying they knew,' affirming she'd be with me in a moment.

By the time I sat down to look at her across the desk, a file with Jono's surname had been created and was waiting. Nadia asked for the transcripts of the phone message and a phone conversation with the Bellingen solicitor, and showed me.

'They've done their homework,' she said, explaining how the public records at the NSW Land Titles Office about her work on the conveyancing of the house sale nine months before would have led them to the only solicitor I'd ever had need of.

'What's happened?' Nadia asked.

I gave her the recap, knowing that the clock is always ticking in a solicitor's office. She immediately came to the same conclusion that I had — I could simply apply to the NSW Attorney-General's office to access Jono's death certificate independently. If there was a problem, Nadia's status as a registered solicitor overseeing the acquittal of a deceased estate would overcome it.

We went through the salient points: Jono left no will. How did I know? He'd told me, and I'd moved house with him four times in five years. Our paperwork was combined. I knew it backwards. No will meant everything that was Jono's reverted to me automatically. It had been that way in the state of NSW for five years previously as far as same-sex couples were concerned.

When Jono's father's death came into the mix, Nadia's face got a little graver. This confused things, because probate had not been granted to Joe's beneficiaries (of which Jono was one, sharing with Maureen and Warren) before Jono died.

'This must be why they're causing trouble,' she said. 'Anyway, this is a case of two estates, not one, and Jono's estate starts with his death certificate.'

Wrapping up by reminding me that an affordable meeting with her would always be a short one, she said she'd get back to me when she'd secured Jono's death certificate.

Blinking in the sunlight outside, and from the shock of suddenly finding myself in litigation, I went shopping.

Back at Claudia and Murray's place, after-school energies gave way to the idea of dinner. Claudia was nowhere to be found, so I made an enormous meal.

Murray was happy to sit and talk with me while I cooked. He and I had not really had time to speak since Jono died, and he seemed very happy for me to be there, contributing to the household with boxes of groceries and a meal for everyone. I asked Bill to set the table, and when dinner was almost ready, Claudia appeared.

We had been the best of friends for six years at that point, so I knew her moods backwards, but this one had an edge. She floated in between the domestic processes occurring despite her absence, noticed the meal, looked at her partner, and then at me, with a kind of serene shock.

It was unnerving. She declined our invitation to join us, and disappeared upstairs. The rest of us ate, cleared up, and retreated into the four corners of the enormous house, which fell into a kind of hand-over-mouth hush quite early.

I was tired, so I didn't stay up, just got into bed and let the shocks of the day wash over me.

In the morning, things were immediately awkward. Murray walked into the living room with Claudia at his side, and they asked me to sit down. I was wiping up some of the dishes from the night before, and just asked them to say what they needed.

'How long do you intend to stay here Mike?' Murray asked. Claudia was looking at the floor.

It was the unfairest of questions. This was the moment I had avoided so long by saying no to their generous request to have me stay with them, and maintaining my distance; yet now, there I was, right in the middle of a swift betrayal.

'And how much rent are you prepared to pay while you're here?'

'You know I am still paying all the rent at Kogarah Bay?' I asked.

Neither of them acknowledged that reality. 'It looks as though I am not going to be let out of our lease until they find a new tenant. I can't answer your question, with that hanging over my head.'

'You have to pay something, and give us some idea of how long you'll be here,' Claudia said, facing the conversation finally, and throwing pain into it.

I put the towel down, and said I would sort things out so that I would not be staying there another night. They both moved to protest, but I held my hand up to silence them.

'I will sort it out, don't worry about it, I'll be gone sometime today, and find out some way of getting my things out by the end of the week.'

Then I went for a walk with the dogs, whose gentle energy galvanised me into action that stopped any useless tears. We had not finished moving yet. Where we would be going I had no idea.

When I came back, Murray had gone to work and Claudia was hiding upstairs. I called my sister and said she was not to ask me why, but I needed to move that very day, could she please ring Naumi, who lived a five-minute drive away, and let her know what had transpired.

Jen didn't tell me at that time, in order to prevent my fragile grip on things from completely collapsing, that Claudia had called her the night before in a state of agitation, claiming I had locked myself in my room and that I was playing my music so loud that Sam couldn't get to sleep.

That silent house, in which I had fallen asleep no later than eight o'clock, behind a door which could not be 'locked' and on which nobody had knocked, was not a place of disquiet, except within Claudia's lying consciousness.

I packed a few bags and had the dogs' things ready when Naumi rang. She said don't worry about anything, just come, everything could be sorted out later, and she had a lead on a granny flat on the other side of town which another friend needed a tenant for, and fast. That sounded hopeful, so I removed as much as I could from that occupied house which was tragically really empty, and got away.

Nadia rang with the news that she had been denied access to Jono's death certificate by the NSW Registry of Births, Deaths and Marriages.

On the phone she sounded annoyed, but in person she was deeply angry, on the edge of offence, when I saw her later that morning.

She'd worked out what I had not up to that stage: that my name had been completely removed from the process of creating Jono's death certificate, meaning there was no way I could access it by applying for one on my own, and, because ours had been a same-sex relationship, neither could a licensed solicitor acting on behalf of Jono's next-of-kin — me.

She said she'd keep trying and get back to me.

I said I didn't know where that would be, because I was in the process of moving, again.

'Again?' she said.

'Don't ask me, please,' I said.

'Oh, Michael ...' she said.

'I'm okay, there's somewhere I might be able to stay.'

That afternoon, Naumi and I went around to see Annie's granny flat.

I knew Annie from the local arts community. She was not there, but her son was, and he showed us out into the back garden, where the 'Little House', as they called it, sat behind the garage.

I liked it even before spotting it, because nobody could see it was there, and, with five-foot-high solid timber fences and an enormous yard the dogs would be safe.

Seeing the three rooms inside was just a formality. I said I'd take it. When could I move in?

We took the dogs around to Naumi's. She sensed they were getting confused and I might be about to break. She told me Jen had booked a truck and was bringing it up in a few days, and everyone would help move my stuff from Claudia and Murray's around to Annie's.

I'd been given a massage voucher which I had already used to book a session that afternoon, and Naumi said she'd watch the dogs while I went to the house at the agreed time.

As soon as the masseur touched the centre of my upper back, my soul opened and out flooded a wave of tears and snot.

Very respectfully, she placed a bucket filled with paper towel beneath my face, which poked through the massage table. The pain was really starting to show, and I felt I needed to explain.

'I've lost my partner,' I cried, 'and my best friend.'

The masseur's face was overcome with a sudden incomprehension, assuming they had both died. Thinking she must not have heard me correctly, I went to clarify, but realised there was no point, it may as well have been the truth.

A DAY later I called Murray to ask if I could get some more things from their house. Nadia had asked me to start taking notes about my relationship with Jono, and I'd embarked using Claudia's computer, but I didn't want to leave that document with people I felt I could no longer trust.

Murray was working somewhere onsite and said he'd tell Claudia I'd be around about midday, giving her a chance to be out of the house if she didn't want to see me.

When I arrived, I knocked, although I had a key, and when there was no answer I let myself in.

Claudia was sitting with Sam in her arms on one of the big lounges in the centre of the main living room. I went to speak, but there was a shield of energy around her.

I grabbed a few things from my room, took to the stairs, and deleted the file off her computer. As I returned along the landing, the living room below revealed little Sam, who locked eyes with me and smiled. Claudia gazed at the view with dead eyes.

I'd forgotten that face. I had only seen it once before, when Claudia crept back into my house years before after falling off the wagon. It was the look of the drug-frozen, 'clean', yet substances still coursed through her veins enough for easy promises about getting off whatever she'd been on.

I'd had so much faith in Claudia that her addictions had completely slipped my mind when it came to living under the same roof. The last time we'd shared a home, she'd gone from booze to heroin. Now, faced with the reality of me, she seemed to be threatening to take up whatever substance or behaviour came next.

Leaving was the kindest thing I could do for her in that moment.

THE last time I'd had anything to do with the NSW Registry of Births, Deaths and Marriages, I'd gone to their archive in Sydney seeking my younger brother's death certificate.

Nicholas had been dead for twenty years by that time, but the loss of that baby still troubled me. I was a child of three when he died, yet I remembered Nicholas well, and the morning Andrew and I had been unable to wake him, a fact we guilelessly told our parents in their bedroom minutes later.

I also remembered Mum's swift response: throwing the sheets off and rushing into the baby's room; then the shocking sound she made as she held his dead body against her neck, keening like a confused gull, unable to temper her response as two wide-eyed little boys stood and watched their father winding the old party line telephone into life to seek help that did not come.

We drove from our lonely farmhouse into Inverell with the dead baby swaddled in his bassinet on the back seat between me and Andrew.

Losing Nicholas, and our inability to discuss it, wrought great damage. Mum and Dad had another baby — Jen — and we all felt recovered; but underneath, things rotted quickly.

Mum eventually manifested confusing behaviour that got her arrested and tried on shoplifting charges. Only a psychologist's report kept her out of the women's prison a day's drive from her family, but my parents' marriage did not survive the fallout.

Without Dad, we moved to the Blue Mountains and made the best new life we could.

By the time Mum's cancer was found, seventeen years after Nicholas' death, her medical teams seemed to look at every possible source of her illness apart from an option that seemed clear to me — the unexplained permanent end to her menstruation, which manifested when she was just thirty-seven, very soon after Jen was born.

Within eighteen months of her exploratory surgery, she was dead, and we were left with only the possibility her primary cancer had been ovarian.

So much family mystery was wrapped up in these events. I sought answers from relatives and friends who recalled the way life had coasted along for a few years. Dad said he'd tried to focus on the living, not the dead, but in that he seemed to have failed and quickly given up.

I decided to apply for Nicholas' death certificate because there wasn't a copy in any of Mum's paperwork. All she kept of him were a few photographs and one tiny knitted suit and booties, which I'd discovered wrapped in her wedding veil in the bottom drawer of the garden shed after her death. Comparing the clothes with the photographs confirmed they were Nicholas'.

At the Registry archives, applying for my brother's death certificate was a simple administrative process. My name was on Mum's death certificate, with Nicholas', because we'd created the document properly. I only needed to identify myself to receive a full original of it in thirty minutes.

On it was a very sad discovery — Nicholas had been buried the day after his death.

But there was more. From the day of his funeral, to the creation of the document I recovered, there had been a seven-week gap in which time a police investigation had taken place.

Mum told me when I was old enough about the police coming to our farmhouse outside Delungra to interview her. Not Dad, just her. That was why she was listed as the informant on her third son's death certificate.

It must have felt so fast, the journey her baby took from her arms to the grave in just one rotation of the Earth, like Nicholas hadn't even been there in the first place; followed by a seven weeks of not knowing what really happened, with nothing concrete to show for her innocence.

Even when Nicholas' death certificate was finally issued, the cause listed as 'cot death syndrome' after an inquest was dispensed with, that one piece of paper never freed her from the guilt of being singled out.

And so, four years later, the police came all the way out to the farm to investigate her again. That time there was an inescapable charge — shoplifting.

At first, it had been kitchen items, then it was children's clothing, the behaviour escalating until someone was courageous enough to heed the cry for help.

With the primary evidence of my brother's death certificate, many of the family myths about this death and the reasons my parents' marriage ended came crashing down.

Three decades later, I was coming to terms with how impossible it is to get someone's original certificate when all references to you have been kept off it.

THE approaching weekend brought cold conditions to the mountains. Jen came and stayed the Friday night at Naumi's and we sat around the fire of an accepting home with Naumi's kids.

On the Saturday, Claudia and Murray and the family were not there. The box of groceries I'd bought in good faith was sitting in the middle of the room, like a challenge. We quickly moved everything out. I left the box and a challenge of my own: fifty dollars for phone calls, despite having made only a few.

While I was vacuuming the new carpet, Jen said: 'Let's go, we've done enough here.'

Over at Annie's we got everything in quickly. I still hold a mental picture of Annie wielding a vacuum cleaner on things that were covered with fluff from the removal truck as they were carried in. It was a lovely practical symbol of welcome.

The turquoise woollen curtains Jono and I had bought for the Kogarah Bay house fitted perfectly over the large glass doors of the Little House, keeping out the cold but also sheltering me against the approaching storm.

SEVEN

THE IRONY OF my short stay at Claudia and Murray's was that the property manager of the house at Kogarah Bay managed to find another tenant to take on the lease very soon after I moved out.

That freed me from paying city prices for a house I wasn't living in, and would have allowed me to pay weekly rent to Claudia and Murray, had they been a little more patient.

I called to thank Tony, the estate agent, and make arrangements to collect my rental bond, a sum of money that would go a long way to paying the rent on Annie's granny flat while I was not working.

He seemed chirpy about things, having inspected the way Jen left the house in a clean, serviceable state, and announced my share of the bond was on its way to me in the form of a cheque.

'And Jono's share?' I asked.

'Well, that's going to his mother,' he replied, as though it was the most natural thing in the world.

'But I was Jono's de-facto spouse,' I replied, 'he left no will, so everything that was his automatically passes to me. Has Maureen contacted you?'

'Yes,' Tony said, suddenly less animated.

'Well, she has no business doing so. The tenancy agreement was between me, Jono, and the landlord. I represent Jono's interests here. I am his next-of-kin,' I replied, gradually finding my voice.

'Well, I am not sure about that,' Tony replied.

'It's the law of the state of NSW, it has been that way for gay couples since 1999,' I asserted.

Jono and I had made the odd joke about Tony. Judging by his demeanour, it was obvious to us he was gay. He and his partner ran the estate agency through which we'd found our 'holiday house' in the city. They'd been a little curious about our relationship, in that manner some gay men employ, seeking to know if a couple is monogamous, or not.

Now, I seriously doubted he was an ally of any kind, simply because I didn't know whether he stood for LGBTIQA+ equality of any kind. There had been no legal protections when his generation was my age, and many of them had long ago given up on pushing for their rights.

He was a 'Friend of Dorothy', from the days when his sexual expression was illegal and hidden away behind secret passwords that gave access to shadowy clubs where men could meet.

Now, in the era of burgeoning equality, me and Tony, both homosexual men, were at cross purposes.

What could it have been which had so quickly persuaded him that my spouse's share of our common household finances was to be returned to Jono's mother and not to his spouse? It was the first of many such betrayals.

I called all the utility companies about returning the deposits Jono and I had paid.

The gas company was an eye opener. They'd already written a cheque and posted it to Maureen, weeks before. I was outraged and asked to speak to a manager, to whom I explained the law as clearly as I could, my anger and grief rising from the deepening hurt.

'But she is his mother,' the woman at the other end of the line stated to me, as though it were the ultimate *fait accompli*.

I tried to explain the laws that defined 'next-of-kin' and 'de-facto relationship', the eleven criteria that underpinned the latter in NSW legislation, and the possibility of any combination of those proving the existence of a relationship as legally binding than the obvious biology of a mother-son relationship, but she would not listen.

In all cases, cheques had been issued to Maureen in Jono's name.

I called Nadia. She contacted Maureen's solicitor in Bellingen and requested all cheques be held without being banked. Added to the rental bond, the total was an amount I could have lived on for a few months.

That this money was being held against my will, pending the outcome of litigation I had not instigated, cut me to the core.

Nadia asked me to come into the office to consolidate some kind of plan. She was always efficient to reduce my costs, but this time she indulged me with time that she told me she would not be charging me for, and looked me in the eye.

'I am outraged!' she said, raising her voice, 'I have taken advice on your situation, and the laws are quite clear. Because they are issued in Jono's name, the only person on this planet who is permitted to present those cheques to a bank is you.'

I imagined every client in every law office on the planet wants to hear that kind of anger from their legal advocate.

'We can only act on your instructions,' Nadia explained, 'you don't have to do anything, but you can apply for what is called letters of administration to handle Jono's estate. That's how an estate is created when someone does not leave a will.'

That sounded exactly like something I wanted — an authoritarian energy to come down irrefutably on Maureen to make her stop the courses of action she was taking.

'I'd like to do that,' I said.

'Right,' Nadia said. 'We are not sure if we can present an application to the Supreme Court without Jono's death certificate, but we can certainly try.'

WHAT I sorely needed in those weeks was Jono, the one thing I could not have. I could have done with his calm approach and his intervention.

Shock had brought me to my knees, so I did something I had not done for a very, very long time — I reached out to members of my disparate family. Remembering Dad's offer to call him if I needed to, I picked up the phone.

Our conversations had been stilted for more than twenty years, but I answered his questions truthfully and told him about the unfolding dramas.

He focussed on my cancelled trip to Europe.

'Just go,' he said, as though it would be easy to find someone to mind two energetic working dogs in time to salvage my ticket; and no problem to land myself in another country by myself, in an acute state of grief, with friends I had not seen in five years. *Typical Dad, suggesting escape from responsibility as the solution*, I thought.

On the day when it became clear I'd need Jono's death certificate to apply for his superannuation death benefit, I felt helpless enough to call my older brother Andrew.

He'd been awkward about my sexuality in the light of his Christianity ever since I came out, but although he was confronted by my situation, he said: 'Just apply for it' when I told him about the problems accessing Jono's superannuation.

Surely Andrew was correct: Jono's death could be proven by other means.

I relaxed a moment and sat back on the pillows at the head of my bed, and felt a genuine sense of fraternal camaraderie. It was very moving, and I thanked my brother, saying that even though we'd had our differences over the years it meant a lot that he was listening and helping me now.

But within another minute, he'd wrapped up the conversation and was not in touch for a very long time.

UNDOING Maureen's betrayal became my focus, but when I was honest with myself, I realised I should have seen it coming.

Not long before Jono died, we walked the dogs along the nearby Botany Bay foreshore. Maureen was due to stay with us the next day.

The previous time we'd all been under the same roof had ended in a terrible argument, when Maureen had been drunk after downing two bottles of red wine, solo.

Back then, the argument was started when Tully, our youngest dog, had jumped onto the kitchen bench and eaten the yoghurt dip Maureen had just made. Maureen was an excellent cook, but also very protective about the manner in which her meals were served.

Nevertheless, after Jono and I disciplined Tully in our way, which was to isolate her immediately after she'd done something wrong, we had a bit of a chuckle about our puppy managing to get up and snaffle the hors d'oeuvres.

Maureen didn't take it well. She began to rant about how lax we were as dog owners, primarily about feeding. According to her, we starved our dogs needlessly. There could be no other reason that Tully had been drawn to eat the yoghurt dip.

I retreated to the living room without saying anything. Maureen followed, and she kept up the rant. I suggested we agree to disagree, but she brushed that aside. I said that if she wanted to pursue it, she needed to be very sure she wanted an argument right there and then.

She brought it on.

So I asserted that we fed our dogs enough, and it was really none of her business. That gave Maureen the ignition she wanted, and she proceeded to march up and down the hallway, admonishing us both.

Jono tried to intervene by stating that he supported me in what I was saying — that we fed the dogs in the evening, not three times a day. He was also brave enough to suggest that the way his mother insisted they feed the Labradors they'd owned when Jono was a child was the answer to the mystery of why the pair scratched themselves incessantly all their lives.

Jono's stance was too much for his mother, and she retreated — with the red wine — into her room.

We sat in the living room and tried to calm down. Jono was upset. He said: 'No one ever speaks to her like that.' I said that she had no right to speak to either of us that way in our own home about the way we lived our lives.

Maureen yelled from the bedroom that she could hear every

word we were saying. I knew at that point that this conflict was not about the dogs.

A year later, sitting by the bay, with Maureen due the next day, I promised Jono I would not engage in any fighting with his mother, I would simply follow through on my first impulse about the yoghurt dip — I would walk away. To avoid her following me, I'd leave the house under some made-up pretext, and Jono would know I was just going to take time out so the situation didn't escalate.

But I also insisted that we collectively consume no more than two bottles of wine at any meal in our home. He agreed, since after the big argument we'd read the material he'd requested from Al-Anon, the support group set up to assist the families of alcoholics.

Quite often when we spoke and things got to the point of arguing, all it ever took was Jono's gentle statement: 'Lighten up, Mikey,' and the rising conflict would be dissipated. He accepted my passion, he accepted my vehement opinions, but he also trusted me enough to be honest and call time on wasted energy.

The absence of him in that regard was fast becoming a source of real grief for me, because I had witnessed the way he'd dealt with his mother and brother in similar ways.

Our peacemaker gone, Maureen, Warren and I were in free fall.

A CUSTOMER service officer at Jono's superannuation fund recommended I start gathering paperwork which would be relevant to the application process, pending the receipt of his death certificate. Now that I had found a place to settle, I started the process of sorting through all the files we'd shared for years.

I might not have had Jono's death certificate yet, but I did have his birth certificate. He'd always kept two copies of it, one of which I gave to Maureen in the bundle of family paperwork Warren had taken away with him, because she'd told me she didn't have one and thought she might have need of it.

It was a very messy document. Jono's name was misspelled 'Jomathan', then crossed out and 'Jonathan' rewritten by hand, initialed and dated two months after his birth. His father, the informant, was recorded with the incorrect initials, also crossed out and corrected.

Jono's surname at birth was not the name he went by for the bulk of his adulthood. Many performers assume a stage name, usually because someone else is already using their birth name and they encounter problems registering with Actors' Equity; but Jono had changed his on a whim in his early twenties.

Maureen's name did not appear on Jono's birth certificate either, because soon after she and Joe went their separate ways, she'd stopped using her first, maiden and married names and assumed an entirely new one: 'Maureen Dae'.

But those mistakes and untruths paled by comparison with a startling omission.

In the certificate section listing Previous Issue Living and Deceased, only Jono's older brother Warren was recorded, above the words 'none deceased'.

But there had been another son — Paul.

Maureen and Joe's first child, Paul had been a very young child when he drowned during a family holiday. His body was never recovered.

According to their own family myths, for whatever reason, Joe and Maureen had never created a death certificate for the lost child.

By the time Jono was born, Paul had become invisible; but as an adult Jono had a shock awakening about a brother he'd never heard about.

'Ask your father' Maureen said when Jono pressed her about the mysterious little boy who made an indelible appearance in the family photograph album.

The rest Jono pieced together for a dance production he choreographed for Bondi Ballet in 2002 — *Lost Brother* — about his discovery of this family secret.

I was there for opening night, and so was Maureen, her pain and grief still held in check, with no bridge to help her from that place, despite seeing the whole experience dramatised.

She and I spoke about death that time, on the two-hour journey from the mountains when I dropped her to the city to travel back to Bellingen. She told me a little about what it was like losing Paul and I told her a little about what it was like for Mum after losing Nicholas, and we discovered a small patch of common ground, a very embryonic sense of familial connection.

Two years later, living alone in Annie's granny flat, I came to understand I was not the first one in their family to be erased from the records.

WHEN Jen encouraged me into grief counselling, I felt unable to keep my energy on anything which did not deliver me fast results. I did not want to be calling around trying to get into some counsellor's office, asked to wait for a space to become available, or have to leave my number for someone to call me back.

Jen understood. I was doing battle, I was emotionally wounded enough and I did not want wishy-washy support, I needed action.

We had met grief counsellors Michael and Wendy over a decade before when they came to our mother's hospital bedside in the days after the doctor announced Mum had only weeks to live. I remembered their courage in listening and not setting agendas, their kindness and their compassion.

They knew Mum well, having worked with her as part of the hospital network, and so we knew them a little too. Jen made the call. Wendy contacted me and set up a time for me to meet Michael.

On the way to that meeting, as I drove down the mountains, my mobile phone rang. I pulled over and took the call. It was Vicki, Nadia's legal secretary. She sounded a little awkward, before telling me that they'd had a call from Maureen's lawyers with a request: I was to cease calling Maureen and demanding Jono's death certificate.

'But I haven't spoken to her,' I protested, 'the last time we spoke on the phone was weeks ago, before all this happened,' I added, remembering how the last phone contact we'd had was Maureen leaving me that awful message on my answering machine about how wrong I was about the equality of same-sex couples under NSW state law.

She had spoken the word *wrong* with such guttural strength to admonish me.

I almost laughed at the ridiculousness of a legal demand for me to cease something I had not been doing, imagining it might have been that Maureen and Warren were panicking in their denial up at Bellingen.

Vicki was sensitive about not adding to my grief at that moment, and assured me they'd provide Maureen's solicitor with a response which referred to the truth: neither client in this litigation was communicating outside their legal representatives.

As I descended the mountains to meet Michael, something about the height and the complete lack of other cars made me shout out loud: 'Sparked your guilt, Maureen?'

In the waiting room I hid beneath my bulky ski jacket, the type with the zip that enclosed a wide collar into something akin to a neck brace. It felt safe.

Michael greeted me and showed me into a room. I didn't know where to begin. He kept it simple by asking me what I had done that day. I told him about the phone call with Vicki.

'I want all this nonsense to stop, so I can start grieving,' I said.

'Michael, this will be your grief,' he said.

EIGHT

WITH A ROLE in *The Dumb Waiter* to learn, I had plenty to keep myself busy.

Creating a character which was not me was a great distraction at that time. I could hide in Gus, Pinter's hapless hitman, as much as I was hiding in Annie's granny flat. His words were written, I didn't have to think of what to say. The fantasy world of the theatre became all-consuming.

Sherreen, the director, was not prepared for the magnitude of what was happening in my private life, which I would reveal only when anyone had the guts to ask.

'I can't help you,' she said, after a considered silence, and though it was a shock to hear it, she was correct. There was nothing others could do to assist me in the unnecessary pain that was coming from Jono's family's denial of my relationship with him.

I'd asked Judy and Jen to organise a series of statutory declarations from friends and family, warranting the existence of our relationship. This was a more painful process than it should have been because it was very difficult to impart the need for this to many people.

But no one can deny your relationship, was a common response from those who could not immediately absorb why I was asking them for written support, often with a disbelieving laugh at the end of the statement.

Well, yes they can, and they are, I wanted to say, quickly exhausted by the inability to show them in some meaningful, immediate way that what they were being asked was both urgent and should probably be done without question, especially if they genuinely wanted to help me.

Endless frozen meals and getting stuck with other peoples' plastic containers are hallmarks of grief in the society we have structured for ourselves. When I asked some for more than a casserole, I started to lose support instead of gaining it.

Everyone responds differently to death developed into a mantra around me that winter.

It was a handy answer plenty of people gave me when I attempted to explain the situation I was in. Far easier to say that than accept what I was telling them about Jono's mother, spilling her pain throughout the remains of my life.

Should a platitude be offered to one grieving person and not applied to another, pining for the loss of the same person? I started to feel a sense of competition about grief, because others had begun to decide that there was a scale of need around losing Jono.

My heartache and confusion at the amputation of Jono's departure told me the truth was very different.

A grieving mother gets a blank cheque. A grieving gay spouse has limits imposed.

It's deeply unfair and ignorant to suppose this division is some kind of universal truth. Hearing and sensing it among my friends was a devastating awakening.

The journey is akin to train travel. Around the time of a funeral, everyone farewells the grieving at an imaginary platform, their destination unknown. A few brave souls board the carriage. Some get off at the first stop. Some hang on for a few more stations, then alight. Very quickly, the grieving are left with few travelling companions.

This will be your grief, Michael.

AS the weeks passed I swung from hope to despair about ever seeing Jono's death certificate.

Warren rang me on my brand new mobile phone, an action which got him right into my safe place in Annie's granny flat, a shock only because I had no idea how he'd gotten my new phone number.

He was pumped up and arrogant, which rendered me calm and full of clarity.

'How are you both?' I asked, a knee-jerk opener.

'Not very happy, we're not happy at all up here, actually,' Warren replied awkwardly. 'Why all this about the death certificate?'

'Well, I have a right to it, Warren,' I said.

'We're not even sure why Jono died,' he replied, the old excuse.

'It doesn't matter, I know there has been a death certificate created. Jono and I were de-facto spouses, and I am not happy about all the denial of that,' I ventured.

The truth was too much and he hung up on me.

A short time after that, a photocopy of Jono's death certificate arrived at Nadia's office from Maureen and Warren's solicitor at Bellingen, finally allowing me to see it for the first time, months after Jono's death.

At last, the lies were revealed.

The first was his family surname, listed with the one he'd stopped using half his lifetime ago. Under Usual Occupation he was documented as 'dancer', a career he'd moved on from years before.

The Marital Status at Date of Death section contained one word: single.

Maureen's name didn't appear anywhere. Instead of 'Maureen

Dae', she was listed under the name of the young woman who'd married Joe at the end of World War Two, and never separated.

Cause of Death was correctly listed as 'unknown'. The NSW Coroner was still waiting on toxicology reports on tissue samples taken from Jono's body during the autopsy.

Then, the Informant: Maureen, again, under her old name, again.

The only thing which connected this disappointing document to me was the address Jono and I shared at Kogarah Bay.

A crumpled photocopy of a certificate which meant so much to me was mean-spirited. It was meant to drive a wedge between me and Jono, and legally it had already done so.

The Supreme Court would not accept a photocopy, Maureen and Warren knew that. Nadia watched my disbelief as I looked up from the paper and cast it onto her desk.

'They could have listed you as Informant if nothing else,' she said, 'not doing that proves an intent to exclude you from the document altogether,' she added, her case building.

I nodded, remembering how disappointed I'd been when I'd first seen Mum's death certificate and noticed my older brother's name on it as Informant. I'd been the one who'd done all the talking at the funeral director's, the one who'd led our grief-stricken family into action for Mum, bringing her home to die instead of allowing a career nurse to see out her last days at her workplace.

In the absence of a clear directive, the role of Informant went to Andrew, although he'd done about as little informing as he could get away with around Mum's death.

But that untruth had been borne of assumptions. Jono's death certificate was a record of lies.

Meanwhile, my copy of it languished in the safe at the funeral home. Luke had long ceased communicating. His spinelessness annoyed the shit out of me, so I was happy to move on to his boss Wayne, who presented with a dispassionate approach to the matter that initially gave me hope he would simply release my copy to me and allow me to get on with sorting out Jono's affairs.

That hope disappeared when it became apparent he was also talking with Maureen and her solicitor. Wayne told me I should 'do my worst' through legal processes to get hold of my certificate.

But there was one thing in those curt discussions that validated me, and that was the very existence of a second original certificate.

Various dissembling phone calls between Nadia and Miko, Maureen's lawyer, had been unable to uphold my version of events — that while sitting with Luke, Maureen and Warren in the home Jono and I shared, when we created the funeral contract, it had been agreed that two death certificates would be created.

When I challenged Wayne to explain why one original death certificate had been created for me if I was not Jono's next-of-kin, he repeated Luke's line: 'Well, his mother says differently.'

Friends have often told me I should have been a lawyer. It was that part of me which helped me through barriers by asking the right questions. In Wayne's case, my line of enquiry led him to reveal, inadvertently, that Jono's funeral account had not yet been paid.

This came as a surprise to me because Maureen had already closed Jono's bank account. According to the bank manager at the Bellingen branch, she'd been able to do this with his interim death certificate on the premise of paying for his funeral with the fifteen-hundred dollars left in the account, money that was legally mine. But this new information showed she had not subsequently used the money to pay the funeral bill at all.

At the time of this phone conversation, I was walking the dogs through the local cemetery, surrounded by the remains of loved ones and the stone remnants of grief. I stopped and asked Wayne to clarify that he'd just told me the funeral account was still outstanding.

He did, with a sense that he envisaged all this fighting was going to result in it never being paid.

So I offered to pay the balance that day with one condition — that my copy of the death certificate be released to me beforehand, which is the course of events for all funeral contracts in the country.

The funeral contract had been created between Wayne's company and me. My signature was on the paperwork.

Wayne could simply have given me his company's bank details. I had just enough money, including the fifteen-hundred dollars from Maureen. That would make things legal, and fair.

It was the ultimate failure of this company — recommended to me because apparently they had an understanding of the needs of same-sex couples — when Wayne ran scared from his final opportunity to make good for me and Jono.

But I knew another person in the chain of events — Nicki, the funeral director who'd acquitted Jono's father's funeral — the one who'd recommended Luke and his company. Before she even knew why I'd called, Nicki inadvertently revealed what Luke had told her about the encounter with Maureen and Warren. He'd been so upset he'd called Nicki immediately afterwards.

'They said something like: *We know why you would think they were partners, but they were not,*' Nicki recalled, and confirmed Luke had told her: 'They bullied me.'

Suddenly I realised what Maureen must have told them. Separate rooms as a relationship choice made it very easy for me and Jono to pass as flatmates once he was silenced by death.

Nothing connected us apart from our address on his death certificate. I presented easily as a gold digger with very bad intentions for Maureen's money.

The morning she and Warren had come into my home and Maureen had tried to cancel the Sydney funeral to take her son's body back to Bellingen, after I'd talked her gently down in her grief, they'd searched for Jono's will. When I encouraged them to leave such matters to me, they left, but the rest of us were so busy planning a fantastic tribute to Jono, nobody noticed where they'd gone.

It would have been a short drive into Luke's office from Kogarah Bay. They probably had an appointment, but I imagine Luke was taken by as much surprise as I was at Maureen's first attempt — to get Nicki in on the new deal, the funeral director she and Luke both knew in Bellingen.

I recognised Luke was gay simply by his demeanour, and because Nicki had emphasised on the phone that he would be *very understanding of your particular situation* when she'd pitched his business to me on the phone the day after Jono died.

So I imagine he put in at least a word for me, the man he'd sat with on Jono's bed while I, shaking and grief-stricken, chose which clothes to bury my partner in.

To have copped a bullying, Luke must have put up some resistance.

Warren would have been on hand for that. His mother's bidding was his job. I finally understood Jono's caution around his older brother — the edges of all Warren's behaviour held the stink of bully.

They always presented as a team, Maureen and Warren, barely indistinguishable when trying to work out a response to their *modus operandi*, but now it was all too clear: she demanded and he acted, never questioning the orders.

I imagine Maureen retreated into her grief while Warren emotionally grabbed Luke by the throat: *I can see why you would think they were together, but they were not partners, not the way you think they were.*

Now, I could see the order of events. I'd told them about Jono after eight o'clock the night he died. When Warren called me before eight o'clock the next morning to tell me he and Maureen were on their way to Sydney, he also said he'd informed their family solicitor.

Before they'd even seen their son and brother's body, that solicitor must have either advised them or inspired them about which course of action to take.

But two gay men had upset the plan, when Luke offered me the funeral contract and I signed it, and we'd mutually agreed on the creation of two death certificates.

Maureen and Warren's awkwardness at that meeting in the fabulous Fifties living room was not due to grief alone — it was also disbelief that I had been treated by the funeral director as Jono's surviving spouse.

They had not dared insert the lie about 'flatmates' in that company.

The only option left to them was to take swift, secret, action — to threaten Luke into creating a new funeral contract with them — then go ahead with the whole thing, keeping me off the scent.

The legal side of my brain needed be sure of this to ensure the grief-stricken side did not completely break down, so I called the only other person who was there — Warren's wife Jane.

'I knew what was going on,' she confirmed, 'but there was nothing I could do about it.'

All possible routes to Jono's death certificate were closed to me, and, assuming they were safe from being held accountable, Maureen and Warren removed Jono from the position his father put him in — beneficiary of one-third of all that he owned, including a house in Bellingen.

To do that, they'd signed paperwork for which providing false or misleading information could result in fines and possibly jail time, and 'Maureen Dae' had dropped all signs of estrangement from the husband she'd spent two decades barely tolerating, by assuming her married name again.

They'd bullied, coerced and lied their way through key family, business and legal relationships, and they'd painted me as the villain.

This will be your grief, Michael.

NINE

MY FRIEND AND landlady Annie was an actor, recently divorced and caring enough to acknowledge my grief, yet leave me to my own devices.

She was looking after her son's dog at the time. Part-dingo Jedda was boss, a fact my Border Collie Olive had trouble coming to terms with. Tully happily acquiesced to both, and we'd all go for walks to show the dogs they just had to deal with sharing the expansive yard. Gradually, they grew accustomed to one another.

Annie asked me a favour with a generous reward. She was in rehearsal for a production at the Sydney Theatre Company and needed someone to feed Jedda on the many nights she wouldn't be back in time during the run of the show. I hastily agreed, because it was an excellent salve for dog politics, and Annie offered me a free ticket to opening night.

By the time the evening arrived, it was obvious this was the performance of the year, and as I tentatively made my way into the crowd, I noticed friends and colleagues from my NIDA days. Some I was able to chat with, others seemed familiar but not open.

I'd never done what some call 'foyer work', industry parlance for networking the opening night crowd, letting everyone know you're still around.

We made a fuss of Annie, not least because of her role in the play, but also because it was her birthday, by buying her drinks and chatting with the friendly set, the ones connected to the show in some way.

Some serious directors were hanging out. I found myself talking in groups of high-powered Australian theatre folk. Some I'd been tutored by at NIDA, others I had never met.

One — Lindy, a director I'd loved working with as a student — asked me what I was up to. When I told her I was acting instead of designing, she showed a little glow of pride, since she was also a theatre denizen who'd long refused to be pigeonholed.

Once it came time to leave the bright lights and big city for the relative calm and elemental solace of the Blue Mountains, it was a relief.

I'd been filled with a terrible mixture of hope and fear all evening. Grief was like watching life through a shop window from the darkness outside. There were people I knew in there, leading what seemed like pretty fabulous lives, but I felt condemned to the sidelines.

A LETTER from the NSW Coroner's office informed me the results of the tissue testing of Jono's remains were imminent.

It also assured me counsellors were on hand to interpret any aspect of the results, which would come via post, or that I could attend a consultation with my general practitioner if I preferred.

They arrived, but there was still no cause of death discovered after two months' toxicology.

I read the whole report, which was a study of a deceased forty-four-year-old man. In it were details of the very early stages of various potential maladies that might have seen Jono off had he lived to be eighty, but no primary reason why his heart had simply stopped.

An inquest had been a possibility for nearly six months, but in the light of the evidence of a pre-existing heart condition (the 'heart palpitations' of Jono's last solo trip to Bellingen), the Coroner instructed that Cardiac Arrhythmia be listed as the cause of death.

His death certificate was updated at that point — an amendment to list what took him from me. What I really longed for was an amendment to document the truth of our relationship.

AS the opening night of *The Dumb Waiter* loomed, I tried to muster some celebration for Jen's thirtieth birthday by ordering a cake, a fabulous cake that was great in theory but tasted all wrong.

Around the table at the restaurant, I joined our Sydney family for Jen's get-together, trying to put on the bravest face I could.

My cousin Diane asked how things were going, and I told her the outrageous truth — I was charting my way through the processes of mopping up Jono's affairs, having documents denied to me, and chasing sums of money owing to me which Maureen had claimed.

Diane was outraged on my behalf, and agreed to help get Jono's death certificate out of his family's clutches.

It felt so supportive, over a champagne, but even as we toasted I knew we really had no plan.

What inspired me for a moment was a feeling of family solidarity. A group of related people is a stronger front than a solo cry for help.

Jen, too, was supportive as a sounding board. I never expected her to call anyone and make demands.

She'd witnessed the way I'd gently hosed down Maureen's discomfort about having Jono cremated in Sydney, and we held to our unspoken agreement that we'd patiently work things out through the proper channels.

What other recourse is available to educated, compassionate Westerners, apart from breaking the law?

I WAS about to open a play in which I was playing a hitman, Gus, who, according to Pinter's script, couldn't tie his shoelaces but seemed to have no problem taking people out with a gun.

After my usual approach to rehearsing — getting 'off the book' early, then finding the character through experimentation — it was the arrival of Gus's gun which nailed the whole performance for me.

The weapon had its own scent. It was a real gun which had been fired, and it reminded me of roo shoots when my brother and I were thrust into the caged back of a ute with Dad and bounced around in the dark finding the innocent creatures to spot and shoot. The smell was the scent of mercilessness.

Pinter's plays are great for stage directions, replete with his infamous pauses, but he also leaves the actor plenty of space for their own character choices, and so it was that I added one for Gus.

Part way through this one-act play the hitmen don their gun halters, and I simply took the pistol, stepped towards the end of Gus's bed, and took aim at the wall of the theatre while cocking the gun in the manner the gun instructor had shown me was the way a lazy person (my Gus) would have done.

I can see now who I was taking aim at in that moment, every performance, and why.

I was one of those people often described as 'such a nice person' by old family friends. Ever since, I have cringed and seethed inside, because I was never nice, I was always just a good listener. When I did speak, it usually came out of the blue to people who'd already decided I was their ally.

My siblings and I were also brought up to be respectful of other people, to not take, to not push, and so when I have been pushed in my life, the work of the selfish souls of other people makes no sense to me.

So I kept all the drama on the stage. I felt heard, because the audience was silent while I spoke. I wielded a gun, so I didn't feel so powerless, and I made a great pretence of being okay, making nice, until I could hold on no longer.

Putting a play on is exhausting and enlivening. Having a partner who knows and supports that is one of the most wonderful things, and Jono and I had encouraged one another through plenty of opening nights.

This was my first one without him for a very long time. No one to come home and bitch to, to celebrate with, to keep me on the righteous path of the creative.

That night, we made a great hit. I just couldn't bring myself to take the lonely road up the mountains to the empty granny flat. I turned to the east and hit the city with one clear intention.

During my coming-out process, I had, like many men, found temporary solace in sex on premises venues, or 'saunas', to give them the overblown exotic name which has nothing to do with their pure male raunch.

In the absence of anything else, they also provide emergent gay men a form of sex education.

My first sauna experience was the day I escaped staid Britain and spent a few nights in Paris. I had no idea what was expected of me, where I was supposed to leave my clothes, what I was supposed to wear, just a towel, or, heaven forbid, nothing?

Men go to these places with a silent agreement of anonymity, because, like beats, saunas are not the territory of the 'gay', they are the place where men have sex with men. 'Gay' has very little to do with it.

Nakedness, under the same (usually white) towel is a great leveller, because the married father looks the same as the queerest 'homo' in just a towel. You don't ask what someone's life choices are at a sauna, you just get down to business.

I'd ceased going when Jono and I were together, because I didn't need to. We had one another, and we revelled in our sex life. For me, sex has always been something of an escape, from stress, from fear, from the unknown, and the sensations of pleasure are a shortcut to oblivion. I have never been with a man sexually who thought or acted differently.

There is a code at saunas, but I never knew that where you place your locker key on its wide rubber band indicated what kind of sexual partner you were. I must have confused a few guys in my time.

That night, I was so hungry for oblivion I was not particularly choosy, and went with two random men who joined me in the same cubicle where we devoured one another. It was so extreme that none of us actually climaxed. There was something so desperately needy in me that could not be consoled through orgasm.

I hit the street so early that the weekend papers were out, picked up a copy and saw our review, my hangdog face as Gus was the theatre pick of the week, but I looked lost.

LISA and I went up to Diane's weekender after the show, and my first statutory declaration was waiting on the kitchen table when we arrived. There, laid out, was a legal appraisal of my relationship with Jono. I put it away, because although it was correct, it was confronting.

Lisa was awkward on that holiday. I was brittle, coming back into myself after being Gus. One night, over billiards, Lisa handed me a note saying that she loved me. Not friend love, but romantic love.

I absorbed it, because I was 'nice'. I told her it was okay.

The next day, she cut her foot on an oyster and her bleeding embarrassment showed she, too, was hurting. Jen and I were impatient. We'd been trying to go rowing, anything other than sit and come to terms with the truth: that we'd been duped by bad people.

Lisa and I drove home. I was a growing bundle of grief, in a ball so tight I was about to explode. Lisa had been caring and loving, but I did not want her love, not in that way. My vulnerability had brought out an inappropriate response in her that I didn't know what to do with.

Right on cue, Tully's eye was hurt when I braked too quickly at a traffic light. She was upset and in pain.

When we got home, I flew into a rage, because Jedda growled at my dogs. Annie was out and I should have realised Jedda would be protecting her home. They all fought and I thought Tully had been hurt more.

I started to scream so loud you would have heard me streets away. I needed Lisa but I wanted her gone.

I wanted to make Tully better but I couldn't, it was late on a Sunday. She curled herself up in her bed, shut her eyes on the pain, and went to sleep, a great idea that should have inspired me.

But since I couldn't shoot anyone or fuck anyone or be loved in the way I needed, I decided at the end of that blustering spring day that I would kill myself by throwing myself off a cliff.

Lisa freaked out at my behaviour and went to buy food (much later telling me she had called Jen). During her absence, I started to make firm plans about the act, which scared me at first, but settled steadily in my soul.

I stayed in bed and translated the cliff-jumping plan into a hunger strike in a tent outside Maureen's house. I'd eat only when she came out and gave me Jono's death certificate from her own fucking hands.

If that didn't work I'd do the cliff, a dog under each arm, and I would tell no one so nobody had to find me.

THE grieving have only one choice to make — to escape death, or be absorbed by it.

It might be drugs, drink, pining away, not eating, or suicide, but if we are not careful when we grieve, or others are not careful with us, we are as prone to death as those we have lost.

Jono died a mere six weeks after his father. Mum could not shake off the death of one of her babies.

To escape death means we have a fight on our hands, and I, too, decided to fight. It hurt, it was risky, but I had to start with those close to me.

Lisa had come back from Canberra for our weekend away to the coast, and she'd brought with her a book about grief which she was reading for her own sake, parts of which she shared with me.

One section stood out — a table prefaced by a paragraph about the primal response of animals to the death of their partners.

The writer used the example of a goose, which was observed to take itself into the wilderness on foot after its mate died, and kill itself by bashing its head against a clump of grass.

The reason was explained in another table, a rather cold breakdown of the impact of loss on the people close to the deceased, configured as a percentage.

At the top of the table was the deceased's partner, with a one-hundred per cent impact (likely to behave like the distraught goose). This was followed by high percentages for the immediate relatives of the deceased, then friends, which warranted a thirty-five per cent rating.

I recall those percentages so clearly, because I communicated them back to Lisa in an email not long after she left at the end of that weekend.

She had brought that information into our lives, and she had shared it with me, but in the light of her profession of love, I felt the need to underline them for her — one-hundred per cent, and thirty-five per cent — an enormous difference.

Even as I wrote I knew it was going to hurt her, that her view of her place on the scale of grief was not down in the thirtieth percentile, but I had to stop being so nice. Being nice was going to kill me, it was clear.

I booked an appointment with Nadia, and got real about what was going to happen. I was not taking instruction from my solicitor, I was instructing her. We were going to apply for letters of administration for Jono's estate.

Even though he died with more than eight-thousand dollars of credit card debt, and despite me having been robbed of my position in his funeral contract, all his assets and liabilities were going to be tabulated, including the funeral expenses, which I would repay to Maureen on receipt of Jono's death certificate.

Nadia flagged that Jono's estate by rights included a one-third share of his father's, even though probate had already been granted, and that I had the right to apply for that.

She also explained that while Maureen was living in Joe's house, no magistrate in the country was ever going to evict her to realise the money that would have passed to Jono, and therefore me.

I realised how claiming that money was going to mean entering into a long-term financial arrangement with Maureen and Warren. I knew in that moment that I would never want that, so I instructed Nadia to leave Jono's share of his father's estate off his list of assets.

She agreed. We went through the list, and she told me we should simply apply to the Supreme Court of NSW with an extract of Jono's death certificate. I was to explain in my affidavit why we were unable to present the original.

Nadia explained what I would need to achieve with this affidavit, that it must outline the whole of our relationship according to the tenets the state of NSW decreed constituted a de-facto coupling. Jono and I met every one of them.

I would have to write the account as though someone was

listening, quoting what Jono and I had said to one another, the various ways we made our relationship public knowledge to both our families and our friends and colleagues.

In my mind I could see what a joyous task this would be, being someone who had made small career inroads as a writer, but also because it was going to put me in touch in an immediate, semi-meditative way, with Jono.

I contacted his superannuation fund again and introduced myself properly to the very friendly customer service team who oversaw the difficult processes of acquitting the death benefits of their clients.

The man assigned to my application did not seem awkward and made no mention of Maureen, he was only interested in helping me access my deceased spouse's financial wish for me.

He also said I didn't have to apply with Jono's mother and brother, I only had to state my case and apply when I was ready, they would handle the rest.

They would not base a decision on the outcome of my application for letters of administration, but they would wait until that was complete before making their own determination.

But there was an obstacle. There was new legislation before Australia's Senate, aimed at allowing surviving same-sex spouses easier access to their deceased partner's death benefits. This man did not have ready access to the progress of the Bill, and advised me to wait and see how the cards fell.

When I faltered in my sense of hope, he wouldn't let me fall. That moment of validation was very important in my escape from death. The man who delivered it never really knew how just a shred of support from someone in authority made all the difference to my shattered sense of security.

I had yet to make a decision on the samples taken from Jono's major organs, used to run long-term tests to determine cause of death. I'd been waiting because I was being nice, thinking that it was something that might be of concern to Maureen and Warren.

So I rang the Coroner's office and spoke to the counsellors who handled bereaved families, and sounded them out about the extent to which I was able to make decisions autonomously about Jono's remains.

The woman at the end of the phone confirmed that they adhered to the NSW state law, which decreed I was Jono's senior next-of-kin, and they were waiting for my instructions about the tiny tissue samples which yielded no answers to Jono's departure.

She indulged my relief at this, and I related what a time I'd had with utility companies, real estate agents and the NSW Attorney-General's department, and she sighed.

'Listen,' she said, 'when the law changed, we got training to update us on such things. That hasn't happened everywhere. They got training in the health system and the hospitals. We are hearing that there are holes in other places about this very issue.'

When I thought back over events, I recalled nobody at the hospital had questioned my relationship; the police had not questioned my relationship.

I thought of all the gay couples in Australia, the many variations of those relationships, all the different ways they may or may not end with the death of one of the partners, and how, once the death had been handled by medical and coronial teams, same-sex attracted people were on our own about the recognition of our relationships, and I despaired.

But not enough to think I was the problem. Not enough to kill myself. I decided that when the time was right, I would do something about this inequality.

I thanked the counsellor for her assistance and support, and wrote giving my permission to have Jono's tissue samples cremated at the Glebe Mortuary.

In a sense, that moment, which happened at a time I was thankfully oblivious, was our final physical farewell, when releasing his mortal remains also released me back into my life.

SOON after, I dreamed of him.

We flew together, high above the vast continent of Australia, him standing behind me, the two of us naked, as we approached the coast at speed. He reached across my shoulder with his neck, drawing his arms wide in front of us both, and the land and sea went calm under the sweep of his hands.

We sped across the coast to the endless ocean, somewhere high above Bellingen, and Jono showed me a vision of a gravestone with someone's name on it, the year of their birth and death.

He passed his hand over the gravestone, and erased those dates away, saying: 'It is not like this, Mikey.'

LISA emailed me, expressing her pain and anger at being labelled by her own book as 'thirty-five per cent friend grief'. I stood my ground when she told me I was to apologise for saying what the writer of the book on grief had told her.

I compassionately said what I was sorry for: that her best, dearest friend was gone, that he would not be able to meet her in Paris for breakfast, like we had all agreed two years before in one of those potentially unattainable life plans, because I was sorry for Lisa on that score, I was deeply, deeply sorry, but there was simply nothing I could do about it other than join the regret.

I also asked her to see a counsellor and tell them exactly what had happened to Jono, but to also have the courage to explain that she had tried a move on a gay man who had lost his partner.

She did not respond.

I kept going to see Michael, my counsellor, and he validated every one of my manoeuvres, let me rail against the insistent attention that all such matters demanded of me, labelling them for the base schoolyard tactics they were — passing notes, whispers, going-behind-backs to get this and that.

And in that manner, I stayed alive. I fed the dogs, walked them, fed myself, and went through the motions of survival, and I did not revisit the notion of following Jono into death.

TEN

TOWARDS THE END of the run of *The Dumb Waiter*, as I drove home up the Blue Mountains, the universe conspired to stop Claudia at the same traffic lights as me. We knew one another's cars so well there was no escaping the meeting, no ignoring it.

I looked across to see if she was holding herself in that terrible frozen state that I had last seen her in, but she was not.

She was looking at me. We asked each other how we were. We both replied. The lights turned green. We went our ways.

Sometime in my new-found survivor's mode, Claudia rang me. There was no moment of reconciliation, only a resumption of the status quo.

But Claudia had given me a piece of music, Coldplay's 'The Scientist'. This was the song she'd played back at our home at Kogarah Bay the night we'd gathered around Jono's coffin in the living room, allowing the reality of what had happened to sink in, but it had not worked for me, I was too numb at the time.

Months later, sequestered in Annie's granny flat after the series of emotional bashings I'd received, I had no barrier against the waves of pain that came vomiting out of me from the deepest places.

By myself, away from the real world, the insistent needs of other people held at bay by the high gate, watched over by three dogs and Annie's respectful distance, I began to mourn Jono.

Real, unfiltered grief had been chased far away, like the frightened goose of Lisa's grief book, whipped by the injuries of others, deep into some insane fairytale wood where there was no solace.

Now, I went on a search and found my goose hiding, broken and near dead, cowering for its very life.

I took it into my arms, felt the fluids of pain running down its feathers, saw how it had injured itself in its flight, how it had been crippled through neglect, knew that it almost did not know its own name, only its own unrelenting shame at being the focus of negative peoples' attentions; robbed, lied about, given a very bad name.

I held it in the darkness, and I pictured Jono, watching from that safe dream place high above the continent; and together, he and I carried that wounded bird back through the woods towards whatever light showed itself.

Only my dogs Olive and Tully heard my cries. At first, they cowered in their beds, their needs taken care of while I attended to mine, but eventually they helped.

Olive was a wild girl, a guardian, the boss lady, and my trembling and blubbering frightened her, but she watched the door as though she would take any intruder, emotional or literal, by the throat.

Tully was the guardian of my heart. She would put one paw on me, monitoring how I was, every bit the nurse, no look of 'end this' on her face, only 'let it come, let it come.'

The exhaustion came quickly each time, making grief as an excuse or explanation for any action after the death of a loved one just something to laugh off.

None of the dissembling, the negative actions, the legal posturing and lies, the lists of things demanded and the sending of a surviving son to harass me in my own home, was borne of Maureen's grief. If she had found a way into her loss of Jono, she would have been, like I was, incapable of a simple line of thought let alone that series of ongoing negative actions.

The tear in my soul was so deep that I had visions of my life being shortened by the scars, and the terrible realisation that there was simply no choice but to go through with it.

This was Yoko Ono banging her head against the tiles at the hospital where John Lennon was declared dead on arrival. My life would never be the same, but yet it would have to *be*. I would have to keep living despite this hole rent in me.

I cried for the lack of Jono, the sheer, unsolvable lack of him, and the tragedy of that for my most selfish self, because we were one another's, we had made that pledge, no matter what any certificate might have said.

I had been fighting for a piece of paper to vainly place it in the way of a bottomless pit.

That realisation was the saddest moment in my life to date, more than the giving up of our future together. The cruel joke was, of course, that we were naive enough to make plans so far reaching as to encompass each other's long-term presence.

In the weary mornings after those nightly sessions, I'd wonder what creatures might have heard me in the night, and if they knew all of us would feel this way, sometime.

I also pondered the great love songs, how their writers warned of this pain, that all of us who were drawn to the lyrics and the music were fooling ourselves if we really believed what we're hearing in such songs is anything other than the sound of approaching pain. Sooner or later it catches up with every one of us.

Yet we are drawn to the flame of love, and the scorching burns it leaves.

Back at Jono's side in the hospital, standing at the edge of the black oblivion inside his eyes, I sensed that I would eventually fall. The question was, how far?

I WROTE my affidavit. I indulged in it. I foreshadowed the legal moment of our meeting with the exciting but nerve-wracking requests for nights out together which neither of us said no to.

I related our first meeting, surrounded by the lies of other men, told in the vain hope of keeping me and Jono apart, and how his car kept breaking down out the front of my house every time he'd tried to drop me home and run nervously back to his own.

The days and dates were easy to recall, because it's rather unforgettable when someone leans their head on your arm and tells you they're besotted with you, hoping that the feeling is mutual.

I recalled the times we encouraged one another to spread our wings creatively, and we pledged to support one another in flight.

The times when we nearly gave up on one another, out of fear, and how neither of us could really manage to. We'd always come together stronger and more able.

I was also drawn to write of Jono's independence as a man, not just as my partner, because I had witnessed and encouraged his emergence, somewhat late, like many out gay men who stand bravely against our parents and siblings to find our true height, our own incomes, our own futures, and our own relationships.

I recorded every quantum leap he'd taken in our years together, every proud stance, every job contract procured and executed, to stamp his independence from those who had tried to claim him in death.

Realising how the arguments with Maureen had started after Jono and I had dared to create a family for ourselves — which did not include her at its centre — I made it clear exactly how and when our trust for one another with credit cards, bank accounts, joint business affairs and dogs had evolved, long before we took the leap and moved in together.

And then I documented his death and the ensuing legal debacle which saw his life partner disenfranchised. I had to, because the Supreme Court would need to know why I was rendered incapable of presenting a crucial support document — Jono's complete original death certificate — and explain why my name did not appear anywhere on it.

It became a compelling statement, much, much stronger than the one piece of paper that was missing, infinitely more filled with the truth — and I was careful to remain completely truthful, determined to trump the lies that had already been told so effectively.

By the time I had finished, Nadia had our application for letters of administration prepared and submitted, and, because the law required us to as a formality, we duly sent it to Maureen's solicitor in Bellingen.

BEFORE the year ended I felt able to work again, but I knew better than to attempt anything too taxing on my time or my emotional state.

Long gone were any of the career plans I had been chasing when Jono died.

In the local newspaper I found an advertisement for aged care workers, with the promise of two or three days' work a week. Not long after I'd applied, I was asked to Penrith for an interview with Sue, who was glad to have a male applicant to place with clients who wanted a male carer.

I duly went for my training, met the other new recruits, all of us at some kind of crossroads: return-to-work mums, older men who'd been made redundant, or those, like me, who hid the real reason we were there for fear of emotional exposure.

I was on a knife edge, and I knew it. Michael, my counsellor, encouraged me to take things very, very gradually.

After basic training about the ageing process, workplace health and safety, and how to wrangle old vacuum cleaners without getting electrocuted, we were all expected to pass a medical examination.

The first one I attended was cancelled when the GP clinic was running so late a swathe of appointments was cancelled.

Accustomed to administrative shortcomings by then, I simply had no tolerance of anything other than top-level and direct communication. I gave it, so I expected it, actually needed it, otherwise I'd have simply stood up, driven home, shut the door and perhaps never emerged.

The second chance for a medical came soon after, and I had to travel a little further to the Western Suburbs.

When I touched my toes, the doctor muttered, 'show off' as he made notes. I shut down, endured the rest of the basic check, which seemed to be more aimed at protecting my new employer from any hidden worker's compensation lawsuits than gauging my general health, and got away.

These moments of interacting with the world outside started a pattern forming in me, which led me to the only form of escape I allowed myself.

As adrift as I was, I was not going to make great boyfriend material for anyone, not for a long time, if ever, so I found myself driving to the only local beat I knew about instead of driving home. Somewhere in there I believed I would find the solace I was seeking.

Greeted at the gateway to the secluded riverside by a rough-looking character with his penis hanging out of his pants, I rushed quickly past and descended into the seclusion of the bush, watching the silhouettes under the trees, away from the midday sun.

I turned a corner to catch my breath, saw a figure shielded by a low hanging branch, smoking. He was tall and that suggested he would be attractive. I approached, and before he looked at me, I realised I knew him.

A sudden rush of guilt washed over me. He knew me and he'd known Jono. We'd debated the real sexual orientation of this married father for years. Suddenly I felt so ashamed of myself and for Jono that I'd landed in this state of ridiculous need.

That was what I felt inside. On the outside, I blabbed: 'What are you doing here?' which was terribly unfeeling, and I wished I could have taken the words back as I spoke them.

He must have felt the same, as he said, looking down: 'Married man's problems', as though it was some kind of excuse.

When his eyes returned to look into mine, they were filled with suggestive hunger. I wanted no part of it, thinking of his wife and whether I'd ever be able to look her in the eye again, and I muttered a few farewells before moving back to the field above.

Up top, I moved towards my car at speed, just wanting to get out of there. A few men were hanging around the toilets, the first place the police would come looking to make random arrests for the illegal behaviour we were all engaging in, every man on his lunch break, or, like me, at a terribly loose end.

Sexual need overcame my guilt, when I told myself I'd just go in for a piss. This created a frisson, when I was followed, and suddenly there was a sense of danger.

By then, I genuinely needed to urinate, and did so, but instead of returning to the daylight I went and stood in a cubicle. A man appeared at the door, just an average Australian bloke, sun-burnished, footy fit with a middle-aged paunch, above black satin shorts which turned me on in a rush.

He hovered, frightened out of his wits, looked at my groin and avoided my face, thought about staying then was gone in a moment, a rabbit dodging a bullet.

STARTING work again gave me focus.

Generally in need of housework, cooking, driving and simple clinical care, most of the time my aged care clients craved only my company, and had usually struggled to get most of their housework done so that I had time to sit with them and share a much-needed conversation.

Most were in acute states of need, the kind of struggle which made my own circumstances seem irrelevant.

My stuff was off limits — carers were not to discuss our private lives. We gave only our first names and never our phone numbers, to stem the great waves of desperation these people were experiencing.

We were warned about being manipulated, coerced by presents and offers of financial assistance. I charted my way through these waters by giving a little extra time and attention when it was safe to do so, and never taxed myself to the point of exhaustion.

Getting out of my own head was very rewarding for my grief, because it gave me perspective, but there were occasions, and clients, whose view of their circumstances was so out of touch with reality they sparked a real hatred from my very worst self, especially when I would have one genuinely needy client who was putting a very brave face on things, followed by a privileged old soul who refused to see how truly lucky they were.

I also sought distraction in another play at the time, a production of Shakespeare's *The Taming of the Shrew* on the riverside in Emu Plains, working with the same director and theatre company.

It seemed a natural extension of the sense of escape that *The Dumb Waiter* had allowed me, although I tried to pretend that I didn't really want to do it, then became rather desperate to win the role of Petruchio from all the others who were vying for it. I was needy about any form of validation.

Other attention came in the form of a very good looking man ten years my junior who'd been part of the backstage crew on *The Dumb Waiter*.

Keen to offer me praise for my performance, comparing me to famous television actors, Dylan's attentions were regular and flattering. He seemed unabashed and totally at ease with my sexuality, respectful of what was happening in my life as a recently widowed gay man, and keen to learn what I knew about acting and auditioning, which wasn't much, really, just a little more than he.

My friend Gabriella was appearing in a play in Sydney, so I cautiously asked Dylan if he wanted to accompany me. He agreed, and after I picked him up from his home on the way, he proceeded to speak of his life in very intimate terms: years of mental health issues, indications of drug use, experimentation of sex with men. All my caring buttons were being pushed.

Gabriella gave me knowing looks meeting us after her show. I stared her down, but was busy gauging whether I would pluck this vulnerable young spunk who seemed to be offering himself up to me on a plate, with his kisses and hugs on leaving my company.

Things became a little clearer, and a little more dangerous, when Dylan admitted he wanted to audition for NIDA that year, and asked me for help.

This was a red flag to my counsellor Michael, who suggested I be very careful lest I not be able to deliver all that this young man expected, citing the schoolyard, again, as the correct way to interpret most human interactions.

I did not immediately listen, and allowed Dylan into the safe world of my granny flat for a lesson in good audition technique. He was too young at the time to know that just turning up and smouldering like a young Marlon Brando meant any drama school would seriously consider him, until he opened his mouth. Consequently, most of my guidance went over his head.

All evening, he seemed to be giving me sexual cues, which I hesitated to take advantage of.

I was trying to show him that what I was offering came with no form of payment expected, financial or otherwise, and he need not drape himself at my feet.

I bundled him out, engaged in one of his breathy hugs in the darkness by his car, and told him I'd see him at rehearsal — I'd encouraged him into taking on a small role in the Shakespeare, even though the language was a challenge.

That weekend, I realised the payment was all the other way around, when Dylan draped himself next to me on the grass, so close that people noticed, and assured me it would be a great delight for me to drop him home, about twenty kilometres out of my way.

There it was, the alarm bell. I said no. He quit the show soon after, leaving me to ponder how I'd nearly been a thirty-four-year-old fool.

I'D grown very wary of some of Jono's old friends. Two of them at Bellingen had gone from the occasional friendly phone call to see how I was, to complete silence and blocking my email address.

I'd explained what Maureen and Warren had done with Jono's death certificate. One friend responded by suggesting I see a shrink, saying I was out of touch with the impact of the death of a child on the parents.

Nice try. I was acutely aware of what a child's death did to a family, so much that I held myself back from direct confrontation with Maureen.

Such was the terrible process of picking teams in the grief game, from people who professed to be enlightened and should have known a lot better.

Amanda had been silent ever since I'd decided not to continue working on Jono's last show. It seemed that others eventually came to the same realisation as me, since *Double Identity* never went onstage, despite me handing over all the ingredients for the willing to carry it to fruition, and stepping out of the way of their plan to go ahead with it.

It became very clear which team Amanda had picked when an email came from her out of the blue, full of challenges: Why did I want a one-third share of Jono's father's estate? Why was I so determined to take all of his superannuation?

Then came the amateur psychology. Surely, Amanda asserted, I was suffering from abandonment issues, and Jono's death was only bringing up unresolved grief I was still carrying from my mother's death twelve years before.

Her penultimate blow revealed more about the case being built against me when Amanda asked me how I expected a 'twenty-two-month live-in relationship' to be a stronger claim on Jono's estate than his mother's.

The contents of my affidavit were obviously being discussed by the band of deniers of my relationship with Jono.

Anyone who felt they had a stake in Jono's life, and there were plenty, was feeding on the legal process.

Amanda's words took me right back to the night Jono died, and the scent of her fur coat at the hospital emergency department, where she'd managed to invite herself into the room — by herself — to see Jono's body, still pliant and covered only by a sheet.

I had no idea in those precious, vulnerable moments that he and I were well and truly owned.

The show-business connections in Jono's life haunted me more than they probably should have, but it was only because he was so vulnerable about them during our years together.

His journal had been written as an attempt to escape those demons.

Long before we met, Jono had turned his back on that part of his life, however, during our relationship, he cautiously returned to the industry, trying to make inroads on his own terms, inviting old theatre comrades back into his life to share the green shoots of his newer, more self-defining work.

I witnessed it unfold, and how their presence was very rarely supportive or generous. Instead, they left Jono angry at their inability to see him in a new light.

There is something potently challenging about a person redefining their own path in front of their former poison playmates, who do what they can to belittle and shame the one trying to change. When these toxic friends do and say nothing, it hurts the most, and that's what I'd seen Jono endure.

While he was alive, Jono was able to protect himself in his gentle, increasingly assertive way, growing in his self-awareness to the point when he realised he didn't need any of these people to achieve what he wanted.

In the last weeks of his life, he was working on what was his last unproduced show, but he was also setting up another production at a large city venue, attending meetings with business managers and negotiating the show's parameters.

I offered to help him with these, but he did not need me. He forged contacts, shook hands on deals, and envisaged the next step completely independently, no showbiz ghosts hanging over him.

But Australia's show-business industry has very strange rules when it comes to gay men. Our stages and our television screens have been replete with same-sex attracted people for decades, very few of them with the support and the strength of character to be out homosexuals.

Deborah Cheetham and Peter Allen are standout examples of out show-business people who forged successful careers despite the homophobia.

Peter Allen played it straight for a while, but that fantasy came crashing down in the wake of his divorce from Liza Minnelli. He returned to Australia, took stock, wrote some of the seminal songs of the 1970s and 1980s, came out publicly and grasped his new-found solo fame with well-deserved pride.

In his own way, Jono had been on a similar journey. He'd retreated from his showbiz career, stated his claim for independence from his family, and in the process manifested a relationship and a new career as a producer and choreographer.

But his death certificate told a different story, because once my name had been removed and his mother's career expectations added, Jono appeared to have died a single dancer. All correct, had he died in 1985.

Amanda's euphemistic comments in her eulogy for Jono finally became clearer when she also made a claim on Jono's heart, trying to leave the impression that they'd been in a relationship.

Jono and I had laughed our way through long driving holidays regaling our sexual adventures before we'd met, and he commended me on my brave attempts to play it straight in a relationship with a woman, something he had never done.

In his journal, he wrote about the same journey in more detail.

'When twenty-one came I decided to get fit. I wanted to do Buckingham (a favourite role) better than ever. I gave up smoking in Bellingen, got my license, grew a stubble beard, got a bit of muscle and tan. I remember feeling all *look at me, I've changed* when I got back to Sydney. At some point I was at Pam's place and began kissing her in the kitchen. I don't know how, it just started. I felt like a man and I felt her boobs, although when she put her hand down on me I pulled away and said I was a Christian! Though putting my hand down her seemed weird too.

'I wrote lovey letters to her from wherever, but it petered out. James (her ex) became more of a fascination for me.'

Other clues about the truth emerged in the script of Jono's first independent production *Show Struck!* in which the character Sherri, a showbiz powerbroker, tries to woo the gay protagonist, Daniel, and has her advances soundly rejected. She is so enraged by the outcome she leaves him to forge a career without her at his side.

Whatever advances Amanda had made on Jono, *Show Struck!* told how things had gone between them.

The end of Peter Allen's closeted contemporaries, who married and fathered children, maintained 'straight' personas and secured a ticket to acceptance from middle Australia, cannot come too soon.

Peter Allen put them all to shame, and they must have gnashed their teeth when he added loving, enduring adult relationships with men to his life's achievements.

Amanda warned me the show-business industry was 'shocked' at what I was 'doing to Jono's mother'.

If any of them had stopped to think, they might have realised

Jono had manifested a partner who cared about him deeply and openly, enough to demand the truth be recorded on his death certificate.

Homophobia often comes from the most unexpected places.

Eleven

THE PROGRESS OF my application to the Supreme Court of NSW for letters of administration to manage Jono's estate was drawn out, and when the response came back from Bellingen that Maureen and Warren were not happy, things slowed right down.

Maureen instructed Miko to put an offer to me, in which I was to give them items — which were not in my possession — and sign away any claim on the estate of Jono's father Joe, which had passed probate while they falsely claimed Jono had no partner and I did not exist.

I pointed out to Nadia this request would surely only be a consideration if Jono's estate assets as listed by us included a claim on his father's estate.

'They probably think we're being very clever,' she said. 'It is possible to amend the asset list before submitting to the Supreme Court.'

To overturn a granted probate in NSW would have been a mammoth, historic achievement, even if I'd wanted to do it, but if Maureen wanted a firm statement from me about it, I was more than happy to give it to her in writing if that allowed me to apply for Jono's estate, acquit his debts properly, and support my access to a share of his superannuation death benefit.

I decided to do what I thought would make it easy on everyone: I agreed to sign whatever document Maureen prepared, at her expense, to warrant that I would make no claim on Joe's estate now, or in the future.

Preparing the letter to that effect was the longest period of time I spent in Nadia's office, as we answered their points one by one, noting where we had already acquiesced to Maureen's needs, and that we would further acquiesce, in return for her agreeing to allow my application to the NSW Supreme Court to proceed.

As the late winter day came to a close, Nadia turned the lights on in her office, and we went over our letter one last time.

I was happy with it, because it acknowledged Maureen's grief while at the same time it made an assertion that she needed to start acknowledging mine. It attempted to end the insistence that I had items of Jono's in my possession that Maureen laid claim to, while at the same time acknowledging the host of items, including her son's ashes, photographs, family documents, clothing and other personal things which I had long ago given her voluntarily.

With great clarity, I accepted her request to sign away any claim on Joe's estate, but I also underlined the truth: that I had never said, written or intimated an interest in making such a claim.

The letter also requested they instruct the funeral director to surrender my copy of Jono's death certificate to me, in return for my signed statement relinquishing Jono's share of his father's estate.

Nadia was satisfied. I was satisfied. She spoke further instructions into a dictaphone for the legal secretary to compile the letter, said it would be sent the next day, and I left.

On the short trip home, an uneasy feeling started to come over me. Why this was, when I was filled from my head to my toes with a sense of clarity, and had asked only for what I needed, was hard to pin down.

I'd slipped into the daily process of shutting the world out by sundown, and made a ritual of watching reruns of *M*A*S*H* to stave off the sense of loneliness and loss. Something about the familiar characters was so comforting, and the comic, wise and gentle manner in which they overcame obstacles was a panacea to all the fuss swirling around me.

Mike Farrell, who played 'B.J' Hunnicutt, also reminded me a little of Jono, both in his demeanour and looks, so this ritual was a small way to feel Jono was at home with me.

The only priority I had was learning my lines for *The Taming of the Shrew* and attending the twice-weekly rehearsals at Penrith. As with *The Dumb Waiter*, it was the perfect way to get out of my own head, even for a few hours, and concentrate on being someone else.

During the week I worked my aged care shifts, which proved a great reminder that I was not the only one in the world with pressing problems.

Life in between the cracks started to prove an eye opener, a place where a dose of good humour went a long way, where even just a small kindness meant a lot.

In many ways, aged care work required another kind of act, that of a 'kind young man' who visited once or twice a week to help 'lovely older people' stay in their homes. I fulfilled roles for them because their own families were often useless, in their eyes at least, and rarely came to visit.

I could see why some families couldn't be seen for dust. Misery and entitlement had robbed many of my clients of their familial connections, forcing them to pay for intergenerational care.

Driving up and down the mountains took its toll on me, and I found I had limited energy most days, so the lighter work hours suited me. Often I'd sleep in the middle of the day to re-energise, before attending an afternoon shift. A state of exhaustion was a hallmark of my grief, but the work also helped me to sleep well at night and stave off the worst of the emotions that stood ready to pounce if I let them in too often.

It wasn't too many days before Nadia called to say she'd received a reply from Maureen's lawyers.

I went into the office. Nadia was busy and said we'd need to keep things short. She left me with the reply in the quietude of a sunny annex, where I read the letter.

I'd anticipated an agreement, and a resolution.

I'd been a fool.

The letter contained two things. The first was news that Maureen had placed a caveat on Jono's estate. It would be very difficult to proceed with that form of legal obstacle.

The second was the confirmation that Maureen had booked a barrister to represent her at the Supreme Court of NSW at a court hearing set in the new year, only weeks away, if I challenged the caveat and proceeded with my claim on Jono's estate.

I dropped my head due to the shock. There was no mention of my multiple offers of conciliation and nothing about my copy of Jono's death certificate. Nadia checked in on me a couple of times, and I must have looked ashen.

When it was my turn, she said there had been a phone call from Miko, Maureen's lawyer, seeking acknowledgement of receipt of this latest letter, and Nadia quoted her offhand comment: 'She also said: *What will it take to wrap this up, today?*'

I asked what that meant, because it sounded like legal weasel words.

'She was asking me what it would take for you to drop all this,' Nadia replied. Her face assumed that comforting outrage she'd so often worn on my behalf. 'I told her that even a little bit of acknowledgement would go a very long way,' she added.

I was losing energy fast. Nadia saw, I realise with hindsight, that our case had reached a pivotal moment, but, as always, she did not want to be seen to be giving me too much time on the books that she'd have to charge me for later, so she bundled me out.

My gut feelings had been right. Maureen did not want agreement. She did not want resolution. She did not want to come to terms with me or my needs. She did not want to give me any acknowledgement whatsoever.

I called Jen and let her know the contents of the letter. She asked me to wait while she wrapped up something important at work, and called me back a short time later.

This kind of desperate phone call had been happening a lot lately. Jen listened, while I related the very latest. This time the import was all the heavier, it was probably designed to be that way.

There was no solution in the moment, only a sense of shared fear and outrage passed between me and my sister. Jen said I should tell my counsellor what had happened.

For six months, Michael had listened to me go over and over the battle with Maureen. He validated my pain and anger, sided with me over her every action and the hurt it dealt me, and understood my lengthy, cogent arguments for why it was causing me pain.

He agreed that the world order was warped if something like this could be allowed to happen.

Jen had been correct, counselling was the only place to take these emotions.

They distracted me, made me see the world, my colleagues in the cast of the play, my clients in their homes, my friends and loved ones, as a host of potential enemies.

I felt I'd run out of options, that there was nowhere to take the fight.

I'd stopped talking to people about it, because I simply could not understand it, and I could not cope with platitudes from those who felt they offered wisdom, but who were as confused and as hopeless as I was about it all.

My next counselling session could not come fast enough.

As I railed at the latest round of nonsensical communication from Jono's mother, moaned at how she wanted to control everything, that she was sticking her nose into matters that were of no concern to her, I posed great unanswerable questions to the universe, searching for the next action I should take to weigh in to the debate once more, with an aim to win.

However, at this crucial moment, Michael stopped listening, and started speaking.

'Why would you want to put your head on that chopping block again?' he asked, with so much calm and sense that it took me completely unawares.

'Well, because she's trying to say that …'

'Why would you want to place your neck onto her chopping block again? You know that she's just going to chop your head off again,' Michael said, very calmly.

I was assaulted with offence at the thought that I should stop doing anything I was doing.

As far as I was concerned, what I was doing was good and right, and what Maureen was doing was bad and wrong.

If she was going to chop my head off again then she was going to be seen to chop my head off again and I would shout to anyone who would listen that she had done it again!

But no one was listening. No one, apart from very close people, gave a shit about it, and even they wished it would go away. I could see it in their kind, water-filled eyes, witnessing my emotional and physical emaciation, as the hurt coursed across me, eating away at me just beneath my thinned skin.

'You could just ignore her,' Michael suggested.

'But how can I, when she is stopping me from doing what I need?' I asked.

'Just step out of the ring,' he said.

I can imagine my face looked flat with shock as I processed this possibility, recalling all the fighting, all the lawyers, all the legal nonsense from Maureen and Warren.

This was the family who shared tips to avoid paying for speeding fines, by paying one cent more than the bill, which meant the amount could not be debited from their account.

If they would fight for one cent, they would fight forever to defend their actions around their son and brother, no matter whether the law was on my side or not.

Michael was offering me an escape route from the bulk of the pain, a portal to another world with as much meaning and as much potential as the vision of my safe meditation place before it had come under duress and was about to collapse. It sounded simple, but it was one of the most challenging emotional steps I have ever been confronted with.

It was a choice, not a fact. It was not like being confronted with Jono's dead body. That, I'd had no choice about. This new place, a place where it didn't matter what Jono's mother and brother did in his name, was undiscovered country to me.

I heard myself saying: *But what about* ... citing some unknown scoreboard, if this indeed was a boxing match between me and Jono's mother.

'You don't have to look at it,' Michael said, 'you can just walk away,' he added.

After all the pain he'd allowed me to share, it must have been a pivotal moment for him to witness.

There would be a term for the kind of person I was if I took this offer, and another term for the kind of person I was if I refused it, if I turned away from it and just decided to fight.

My trouble was I didn't know which I was in that moment.

TWELVE

IN THE LEAD up to the 2004 federal election, the issue of marriage equality hit the media.

The year prior, various provinces followed Ontario's lead in Canada and allowed same-sex marriages to take place. Many Australians availed themselves of this legislation since it did not require the couples to be residents, but as soon as the newlyweds stepped back onto Australian soil, the marriages had no legal standing whatsoever.

Two couples decided to test the Australian *Marriage Act (1961)*, and their application landed on the desk of federal Attorney-General Phillip Ruddock, sending him into a spin.

It turned out there was no specific mention of gender in the Act. As far as the law was concerned, any two people, same-sex or otherwise, could apply to be married in this country. Back in the early 1960s when the legislation was created, nobody even dreamed of marriage equality.

The conservative Liberal government, led by John Howard, went into overdrive to see this loophole changed, and they got plenty of support from both sides of parliament, election year or not.

By August of the year Jono died, marriage equality had been made a legal impossibility in this country. I barely recall the announcement. It would have passed through my consciousness in my deepest grief and registered only as another reason to feel dreadfully unsafe about being same-sex attracted in my own country.

The looming election, of course, required me to turn up at the ballot box, since all Australians must have our names ticked off the voting register on the day, whether we use our vote or not.

The voting queue at the local primary school, the same one I had attended over twenty years prior, was long. It gave me plenty of time to think over the issues, and, more importantly, to observe people and the colour of the how-to-vote cards in their hands.

Prime Minister John Howard was showing great leadership for the majority of Australians — sixty per cent — who objected to marriage equality, and, by the amount of blue of the cards I saw all around me, things were not about to change.

They didn't. The diminutive target John Howard saw off the Labor party's brutish Mark Latham, no problem.

But marriage, like a seed, was planted within me as a concept. Alone, processing the loss of my partner, I pondered what difference marriage would have made to my situation.

First and most obvious was the certification. The warranting of a relationship's existence is so easy with that 'one piece of paper' which straight couples had enjoyed access to for years prior, eschewed by many as either too binding or not needed.

I realised how much simpler it would have been for me, one certificate, and how much harder — impossible — it would have been for Jono's mother and brother to erase the visible signs of his relationship with me.

I thought of the traditional marriage vows, and the words 'forsaking all others'.

I processed its meaning, looked deeper than any sublimation of women and property rights, to find how the line was actually a warning to all those present at a marriage ceremony that they are the forsaken ones. Their son or daughter is placing them on solemn notice with that line, warranting that they are no longer the next-of-kin to their loved one.

Their spouse replaces family, from that moment, and a new family unit is created.

My parents' marriage had ended in acrimonious divorce, to the point where my mother was wary of any signs of my father in me and my brother, and our father allowed his new wife to demonise our mother as she saw fit.

I was glad they did not stay together, and Prime Minister Gough Whitlam's leadership on fault-free divorce through the creation of the *Family Law Act (1975)* had built the firm foundation that allowed many families to undo what needed to be undone, with access to legal aid and counselling.

Almost instantly I shed my wariness of marriage. I saw exactly how it could work for same-sex couples needing that line in the sand around our relationships, whether the marriage lasted forever or not.

Marriage did not have to follow the archetypal plan. Its history is littered with anomalies, of couples stretching its boundaries, simply because they were quite safe, by law, to do so. In recent times, any victim of marriage also had recourse to become unmarried.

I recalled the night Jono and I went out for dinner to our favourite pizzeria on Katoomba Street, on the brink of relocating to Sydney and starting a new phase of our lives.

Jono was pensive until he revealed what was on his mind: he was worried that he did not have enough to offer me as a partner, being ten years my senior. He wondered if I wanted to explore other relationships.

I looked him in the eye, and held his hands between mine, and said: 'No, Jono, that is not what I want. I want to be with you.'

He bent his head in his humble, accepting way, flicked the corners of his mouth up, and we kissed.

From that moment, we were married. The only things missing, apart from the support of any law, were two witnesses and a state-sanctioned celebrant.

Widowed and alone in that voting queue, barely two years later, I became a marriage equality advocate.

WHEN decision time came about pursuing letters of administration for Jono through the Supreme Court, I moved swiftly into new emotional territory.

That 'nice' side of me which dictated I needed to tell people of my decision, particularly Maureen and Warren, was buried very deep.

I let them stew on the outcome of their legal threats and wonder what my next move was, and I imagined them accruing time at more than one law firm and getting charged for it.

Christmas was coming, and I needed to work out what I was doing. Michael cautioned me about getting stuck in awkward situations and feeling overwhelmed, so I was determined to stay at home.

Jen came up from the city with my old friend Christine. We cooked and watched videos, went for walks and talked. I shared my unfolding plan to drop all litigation, and was met with a wave of support.

Later that night, I lay awake and imagined exactly how and when I would do it. It would not be to anyone else's schedule, and I was determined I would not be communicating with Jono's mother or brother anymore.

But before I could feel totally comfortable with my decision, I needed to come to terms with what had inspired Maureen and Warren to drive such a decisive case against my relationship.

Were they only protecting their inheritance, or were these months of lies just garden-variety homophobia?

I imagined what it would be like to witness my relationship with Jono under examination by Maureen and her legal representatives. How would we come under attack if things went that far? Would she have any scruples whatsoever?

Jono had already told me about her reactions to his sexuality, and his journal recounted the same stories.

Of his first unsure and courageous romantic encounter as a teenager, Jono recalled: 'He wrote to me in Sydney — long romantic letters that made me feel repulsed. My mother had read them and showed me in my bedroom that she had. I felt betrayed and found out. She wanted me to see a psychiatrist and said if my father found out he would die. I think I just wanted to run away after that.'

The subject of Jono's sexual orientation was left unspoken for a further twenty years, after he'd returned to Bellingen and was living with his father, and he'd been cast in a short film as a cross-dresser.

'My character got reactions from Mum and Dad. I confronted them about being gay, as no one had actually said they accepted it.

It was a triumph moment and I felt clear and out after that,' he wrote.

Within a page of recording those bookends to his coming out, Jono wrote of moving away from Bellingen to the Blue Mountains, and it was at that point the recollections in his journal ended.

But he'd told me about this 'triumph moment'.

My questioning mind asked for more specifics about his parents' responses. Apparently Joe let out one of his usual exclamations: 'Of course we accept you!'

Knowing Joe and Maureen, I could imagine the way it went — Joe's open-hearted desire to see his son happy filled his estranged wife's silence — because Jono could not remember Maureen's response with any clarity.

There was also her written demand that I sign away all claims to my share of Joe's estate. When I swiftly agreed to this, she didn't even bother to have an agreement drafted up, but moved to block me from applying to the Supreme Court.

So, was she really only worried about money, or was there something more at work?

I'd searched everywhere for answers. The only place left was inside, and I had a strong feeling neither Maureen or Warren had ever earned the right to stand in judgement of Jono and his relationship with me.

I was all that remained of Jono's important life decisions, but I also had financial and emotional needs which the creation of his estate could assuage. Letting go of those meant I had to trust everything I needed would eventually come to me by some other means.

And there are some things for which there is just no answer.

Why would a bereaved mother be homophobic towards her son and try to destroy every record of his relationship? Why would a bereaved mother manifest kleptomania and risk a jail term which would separate her from her surviving children?

Why would a woman try a romantic move on a gay man? Why would someone encourage her best friend to move in, then do everything she could to move him out again after two nights?

Why would a man sexually attracted to men marry a woman and have children, then engage in sex with men in public toilets? Why would a gay man who'd been well-loved seek anonymous sex a month after his partner died?

I only had a half-baked answer to the last question and nothing more, because human experience is littered with more paradox than I was willing to admit.

I'd also heard all the valid-sounding answers.

It was a cry for help. Everyone responds differently. It goes against the laws of nature.

That night, I accepted everyone would think differently about Maureen and Warren's trampling of my human rights. I knew I'd been legally defeated, and how, that was all that mattered. I might never know their reasons, I only saw a way to escape their battle.

I EMAILED Nadia once the holidays were over and instructed her to cease all communication with Miko and any other legal representative for Maureen and Warren. She agreed. There would be no responses given. We were ceasing litigation but we were not telling them anything.

I also asked Nadia to send me the bill for her work.

When it came, the amount made me laugh — fifteen-hundred dollars — the sum of money Maureen had given me in that cheque.

From a financial perspective, Maureen and I were now square. The money had bought me a powerful affidavit which I could now use to apply for Jono's superannuation death benefit.

I described Maureen and Warren to Annie and asked that if they ever turned up at her door she was to say she'd never heard of me. The Little House was totally invisible from the street through a high gate I could lock if I felt vulnerable.

These measures came from a puffed-up heart, but they were healing. I was telling myself and my closest supporters I was ready for these people if they brought their pathetic fight to my doorstep after I'd stepped out of their ring, taken off my gloves and left the building.

THROUGHOUT the year I'd been planning a memorial plaque for Jono. The Sydney Dance Company at Walsh Bay agreed to house it in their main corridor, where dancers daily came and went to rehearsal studios. Jono had worked at and loved this place of movement and anticipation.

I wanted a plaque which expressed itself subtly and was almost not there. A friend and artisan, Sondi, helped me design one out of stainless steel, with a place for one of Jono's tap dancing heels.

His journal yielded some wonderful quotes about his love of dance, the fluid escape he enjoyed within its freedoms, and we had those engraved into the metal, set off by a silhouette of Jono at the peak of a grand jeté, the most iconic of ballet moves for a male soloist and the pinnacle of his achievement with the Australian Ballet.

I planned a small service with Jono's dance friends and mentors. Naumi collected me from rehearsal on the banks of the Nepean River. Christine agreed to be an MC of sorts, to add glue to the little ceremony.

Prudence had been at Jono's first dance school in East Sydney, and she spoke of the talented boy who went off to the Australian Ballet school as a teenager, where Jono met Liz, who recalled the young man who went on to become one of Australia's most inspired young ballet dancers within the newest branch of the company, and danced for audiences across the world.

When it came to me, I went to speak a few words I had jotted down about the man I knew, who'd become a choreographer, because everything about him had remained a dancer and movement expert. It was the language he expressed himself best in.

But I suddenly became incapable of speaking.

Faced with a gathering of friendly faces, I simply couldn't get the words out, overcome by the pent up emotions of the past few months, the sense of disenfranchisement and the unnecessary extra pain inflicted on me by people I was never going to invite to that special memorial.

Annie made a gentle suggestion that I needed to breathe in order to speak. I tried, but no, it wasn't going to happen, then Jen stepped up to the plate, took the paper from my hand, and read it for me.

We looked at the plaque. Liz pronounced it 'sexy', and we all agreed, before taking afternoon tea in the café.

I had ordered a special cheesecake, which Jono and his friends remembered craving while they starved themselves to attain what was thought to be the right shape for ballet, and chuckled to myself at how little of it anyone connected to the dance world ate that day.

But the day was not over. I'd also planned a video night for people to gather and watch clips of Jono's career.

We arrived in a bundle of unresolved emotion. Liz put on a great welcome and delicious food. I silently noted Christine's unnecessary quip about how my sister Jen, if she wanted to lose weight, shouldn't be drinking sugary drinks, and a showbiz friend of Jono's got out the DVDs.

The clips were interesting, but collectively they didn't match the vision I had of Jono's career. In a rush of embarrassment I realised what a terrible mistake the whole idea had been.

I knew the shame he felt about his career, the confusion and frustration of his journey. He'd declined pleasing industry gatekeepers to get auditions, relied on talent alone and therefore got only bit parts here and there, all the while knowing how others got ahead through networking and giving people what they wanted.

He kept his integrity intact through those years, but that meant never got Jono what he called his 'ticket'.

His dance career only amounted to memories of his great achievement as a soloist in *Giselle*, photos of the ensemble piece *Song and Dance* and a few surviving tapes of television work as a backing dancer.

Without him there to moderate the truth, to fill it with his cheeky showbiz nature, it was stark and it was very sad.

During clips of the 1988 Royal Bicentenary Concert, when Jono and every commercial dancer in the country had torn up the stage in one of the greatest displays of Australian dance possibly ever put together, someone mentioned Marcia Hines, who was now back in the spotlight due to her work as one of the judges on *Australian Idol*.

I remembered her in that concert, because she had been missing from the Australian music scene for many years at that time, however, in my memory, Hines was not the vision she had been in the 1970s.

Someone else said what I was thinking: 'She'd put on weight, hadn't she?'

We spooled through to Marcia's concert moment, but no one spoke because she had not put on weight at all, she was just her gifted self in every way. We'd all had our cruel 1980s goggles on.

ONE strong memory of Jono kept me together that night, and it was everything to do with dance. I'd seen him choreographing and demonstrating dance moves many times but one week, when we were living together at Katoomba, we went to a dance class at the old Masonic Hall at the top of our street.

Before the class got underway, we joined the students donning ballet wear and warmed up, all of us with older bodies going through the motions of dance classes from our youth. Our friend Julie was there too, and we formed a slightly nervous trio of newcomers in the corner.

The class started on the easy moves, and we all had a laugh. My funny bone kicked in when things got slightly more complicated — half turns and little leaps. No one cared, it was all meant to be fun.

Then the teacher asked us to line up in the corner to move onto something a lot more complex. She demonstrated a leaping turn and encouraged two of the better dancers to follow. Jono muttered the French phrase of this move, and quietly went into a series of deep stretches.

The good students launched themselves across the diagonal of the hall in amazing feats of expression as they leaped and turned in pairs.

Julie was up there with them, but the skill level diminished with the next group, who fumbled our way across, like clowns. I had barely gathered myself at the far end when the teacher called for Jono and the last student. He had a poised look on his face, his jaw set and his nostrils flared, then he launched into the most graceful crossing that old hall had probably ever seen.

Space and time stopped for a moment, because the move my partner was making was bigger than the room. He'd set his sights on that spirit place all serious dancers know about, high above the mundane world, and, years after he'd done anything similar, his body followed his soul to reclaim his birthright as a figure of grace.

We all fell silent. The teacher, a lithe creature herself, dipped her head in a bow of acknowledgement that this was not taught, it was attained.

If show-business had turned Jono down, there was something terribly wrong with show-business.

I GOT sick soon after, a sore throat which moved to my lungs — my old malady — and then bouts of asthma, all while completing the final rehearsals for *The Taming of the Shrew*, a high-action show with lifts and physical comedy which I was becoming less capable of achieving.

Spending nights down by the river for the show probably didn't help, but I also knew this was grief seeping out of me when I needed it the least.

Shakespeare's hero Petruchio is a complete asshole to his heroine Katharina.

Academics have ignored his misogyny, theatre companies have tried to explain it away or put it into context, but at the end of the day he's a manipulating liar with no reprieve.

During Katharina's famous monologue in the last scene, her right of reply, which packs no feminist punch whatsoever, I decided to eat the fruit on the table in front of me, munching and spitting as rudely as I could.

It was those moments I loved the most, because they were empowering. They did not need to me to speak, I could be as disgusting and as unreasonable as I wanted to be and then I got to stand up and have the last word in the play, dropping all semblance of 'nice'.

HALFWAY through the run my car broke down as I was hurtling along the freeway to the city.

It happened just as I accelerated to the speed limit, and everything just stopped. The dashboard lights went out and the car came to a slow halt on the verge, because the steering locked and the brakes were ineffective. I suppose I was lucky it didn't happen anywhere more dangerous than a four-lane road.

I waited in the sun for a tow truck, which took me to Rooty Hill and a sad-looking car yard.

I got a train home and walked from the station up to Annie's, a walk I took countless times in my youth but which now came with such a sense of thwarting, like I was being made to tread pathways I'd long trodden, in order to learn something.

What more did I need thrust at me right now?

The diagnosis was bad news. A gasket had blown and a new engine was the only solution. The mechanic had already alerted the scrap merchants and gave me a quote for a new engine, or cash for selling the shell of the vehicle. I had no choice but to take the latter option.

Money was getting very low, and now I also couldn't do my aged care work, since I needed a car to get to my client's homes and take them shopping and to medical appointments. This change in my fortunes forced me to focus even more on the progress of my application for Jono's superannuation death benefit.

CHRISTINE had spent the late winter directing a short film she'd also written, and when the time came to screen it, she asked me to arrange a showing with friends in the Blue Mountains, specifically asking for it to be a friendly crowd so that she could grow accustomed to screenings of her government-funded work.

Having made independent films of my own, I knew the feeling, and I leaped at the chance to help.

Claudia and Murray offered the use of the room I had lived in for two nights, by then their television room with an enormous screen, heavy curtains, and vast comfy lounges. It was a home cinema like no other.

Christine agreed to it, then, at the last minute, announced she only had VHS tapes of the film.

'No problem,' I said, 'we'll hire a VHS player from the video store.'

I borrowed Claudia's car, went to collect it, and set it all up so that we could watch the movie that afternoon.

'We don't have to watch it,' Christine announced as she arrived. I knew self sabotage when I saw it, so I decided to ignore her and got the viewing underway.

Christine had two films to show us, a hilarious short which she'd made on a shoestring for a film festival, and her new work, a horror movie. It was moody, frightening, funny and beautifully made.

We all watched with supportive energy. I laughed openly at the first, because of the 'Ab Fab'-style characters and humour. The second film mesmerised us. We watched it twice. It was a glimpse from another world.

Later, trying to get to sleep, Christine talked into the night from the other room, and challenged me on why I did not like her horror film.

I said: 'Don't be ridiculous. It's wonderful!'

When she confessed she thought it wouldn't do anything for her filmmaking career, I added that since it had been funded by the NSW and federal governments, they would ensure their investments — her movie, and her — would be screened and seen at film festivals the world over.

I'd refused to engage in any false flattery or sabotage, and I'd refused to be 'nice' about it, but inside I knew why I had responded more to a short comedy than a horror film.

My life was beyond the indulgent fantasies a horror story weaves around death, loss and the paranormal. The horrors I was facing were all too real.

JEN and I decided we'd take a trip to Canberra for the Easter weekend and stay at a caravan park, just the way we'd done so many times when we were kids when Mum would bundle us all into the car for what she called 'Mum's Mystery Tours'.

The name was funny and we all played along, but in adulthood I came to realise why the first Mum's Mystery Tour was kept a secret: so that none of us could let slip to Dad exactly where we were headed.

She drove us from Inverell to the Blue Mountains to stay with an old nursing friend, via a weekend at Jenolan Caves. On the way home she announced Dad would not be living with us anymore. By the end of the long day's drive we arrived home to a dark house from which half of the furniture had been stolen.

So, a mystery tour was fertile ground for a long weekend's worth of sibling camaraderie. I planned to catch the train to Parramatta where Jen would collect me, and we'd head south to our nation's capital.

On the train I hoisted one of Jono's beloved retro bags into the luggage rack and sat down. I love train travel, and was soon mesmerised by the rocking of the familiar trundle down the hill onto the Sydney Plain.

My thoughts turned to my present situation, and I failed in my attempts to feel good about it, dwelling on Maureen and what she had gotten away with.

I suddenly noticed we were approaching Parramatta station, so I dashed to get off with my shoulder bag, but by the time I was outside and the train had pulled away, I realised I had left Jono's bag, full of my clothes, on the train.

Jen suggested I call State Rail. They said we should go immediately to central railway station in the city, by which time the bag would be handed into lost property.

We dashed to the city's main station, but as we walked onto the main concourse, we were greeted by a terrible sight.

A man had collapsed on the hard floor, his face ashen, eyes open and already dead, with a non-seeing gaze up to the great curved metal ribs of the station roof. Someone had commenced resuscitation and others had pulled a few screens around to shield passers-by from the scene.

Only the screens would never work, because they were signs at eye height, and the man, his death obvious to one who had seen it all before, was lying on the floor where everyone saw but did not want to see.

At lost property there was no sign of my bag, and never was. In it were my favourite clothes, and the sweater Jono had bought on his last lunch break on his last day on the planet.

Another layer of my identity stripped away. Another soul lost to the world.

WHILE we were away, Jen and I had time to talk. So often, our communication had consisted of me calling her in desperate need for solace after the latest disaster, but I'd tried my best to temper that need of late.

Jen had started work with a new company just a fortnight before Jono's death, and they had been very understanding when she'd explained her need to give me time.

'There's really just us,' Jen told me she'd said to her new boss, the awkward truth of our disparate family laid bare to someone she hardly knew.

How long had it been so? Since Mum died, twelve years before, our friendly home had disappeared and our community had altered into a shadow of itself.

The vibrant one, the forgiving, friendly, translator who was our mother, left a swag of confused people in her wake. I'd fallen off many branches when I came out. Jen had fallen off just as many when she did not respond in the 'correct' way to various attempts to give her the kind of succour only her mother could give.

We were an exiled pair, but I was grateful for Jen's constancy. She never told me to get over it, lurched with me from shock to shock, sided with me unquestioningly about all the legal nonsense, and she held back when she could have struck out at the people who were hurting me.

I shared with her how exhausted I felt about Christine's movie screening day, how stepping into the role of creative supporter had come as easily to me as it had always done, but that I now felt uncomfortable about it.

We went to the Museum of Australia and the National Gallery, ate at one expensive and many ridiculously cheap restaurants, and caught glimpses of the trussed up body of Pope John Paul II on our caravan's TV, me wearing the same set of clothes I'd been in for four days, planning to buy more but never quite getting around to it.

The weekend had an edge of humour to it, and a sense of recovery. I got home to Annie's, where she'd watched the dogs for me, with a lighter heart, but I knew I had some emotional work to do.

Feeling equipped to be real with Christine, I emailed her about how drained I'd been by the movie screening episode.

Minutes later, she rang, the disappointment at the loss of her creative support flooded through the phone line, taking full aim at my use of email as the form of communication.

I argued that I was at liberty to communicate with her by any means I wanted.

She disagreed. For her, speaking was the only form of communication for such things. I stuck to my guns, said we were speaking now, and fumbled my way through the conversation.

I related the first time I verbalised something which changed a life, how when I was three years old and didn't realise not being able to wake a baby meant it was dead.

I'd found it almost impossible to deliver important news in person ever since because I could not bear to witness the life altering before my eyes, knowing I was the messenger.

She deftly carved me up with her skilled direct communication, nattily avoiding hearing anything, and announced she needed space.

Our endless battle, played out on my ever-so-slightly recovered life, but even as I sensed her disappearing again, I let Christine go.

Claudia said later she thought Christine had not changed in the years she had not been in our lives, in fact she was probably worse, but I didn't respond.

Our three lives had come a very long way since our brief cohabitation five years before, when I'd served as caretaker and creative champion to them both.

It would not have mattered how I communicated to her — Christine was ready for me to be fully recovered and support her creative journey again. We'd arrived at her station on my grief train, and she had gotten off, whereas I still had a long way to travel.

Thirteen

I WAS IN very new territory. I had no solicitor. I had cut off all communication with Jono's mother and brother, and I wasn't in touch with anyone who'd been in his life before I'd met him.

Life had delivered me a job I could manage while I was in grief, but had taken it away just as swiftly when my car broke down.

I also needed to move from the little sanctuary I'd found in the town where I'd grown up. Annie had put the house on the market as part of her divorce settlement, and a buyer had been found.

My father and brother had observed my grief, but found themselves incapable of helping me.

My sister and two very strong friends — Naumi and Judy — stood by me, all of them keeping their distance and helping when it was practical and achievable to do so.

And I decided to forego the main pursuit I gave myself at this time: the creation of Jono's estate with the Supreme Court of NSW, action that had taken up most of my time, energy and thought.

Usually on waking, I'd mull the non-fighting concept over in my head, running the sense of injustice through my consciousness over and over in the half light, trying to come to terms with it.

I realised I would never come to terms with Maureen and Warren's reasons, so eventually I uncovered another source of anger — this time at Jono — for leaving me prone to his family's warped morals by not making his intentions clear in a will.

Halfway through our relationship, I had changed my will to

include him. He had never in his life made one, and I began to question why.

The one asset he felt he had was his superannuation fund, which had been consolidated over the years into a modest sum with a small amount of money allocated for a death benefit. He'd nominated his mother and me as equal beneficiaries.

Accessing this money became my new focus.

Because I had to move again and I didn't have a job, I needed funds to restart my life on an independent footing, so I picked up the phone.

The customer service officer I'd spoken to months before remembered me and offered some very good news: since I'd been in contact with them, there had been changes made to Commonwealth superannuation legislation — *The Superannuation Industry Supervision Act* — and same-sex de-facto spouses were now on equal footing with our straight counterparts.

I was slightly taken aback, partly because of the Howard government's successful war on marriage equality, but also because I was frightened that regardless of what the law stated, Maureen and Warren would find a way to rob me of what I needed.

I ran through the details of Jono's death, specifically the date, to check if that would rule me out from benefitting from the new legislation. He took a moment to check, but, considering the passage of the law's amendment began on May 27, 2004, four days before Jono's death, his fund was covered by the changes.

He understood that I felt on shaky ground when I explained that it was not possible for me to get more than an extract of Jono's death certificate. Since Maureen would also be applying for her share, he said they would be able to cross-reference my claim with her copy of the original certificate.

I explained I was no longer seeking letters of administration for Jono's estate, that I would be tying up his affairs myself. He said that was no problem, and I should include my affidavit in my application.

In theory, it all sounded easy.

The return from selling my car for scrap, and the money I eventually got back from my travel insurance claim using my affidavit, gave me enough to pay the deposit on a rental in the city.

I could get some sort of job once I got there, and when the superannuation came through I'd have enough behind me to tread carefully about what kind of work, and what amount, I could manage at the one-year mark since Jono's death.

So I completed my application, included the statutory declarations created by friends and family, and all the other documentation that Jono's superannuation fund required, sent it all in, and waited.

The customer service officer said it was all in order, but since there had been no application from Maureen, they were going to contact her to ensure she made one in a timely manner.

It was during this conversation it became clear that even if she applied for a fifty per cent share of her son's superannuation, Maureen was not necessarily going to get any of it.

When I pointed out that Jono had nominated her for a half share, the customer service officer said that might be so, but superannuation death benefits were designed to go to surviving parties who were either partially or fully financially dependent on the deceased at the time of their death.

Parents very rarely fell into that category, unless, for example, they had been living with their deceased children, or their accommodation costs were being paid, even in part, by them.

A week or two later, I contacted them again to see if any application had been made.

The answer was no, but there had been a phone call from Warren. In the egalitarian spirit of superannuation legislation, all applicants were party to communications from all other applicants, and I was told the nature of that phone call.

Warren had asked about the application process, and, crucially, whether creating an estate for Jono with letters of administration from the Supreme Court of NSW would entitle him and his mother to the whole of Jono's death benefit.

I was speechless. The old fighting spirit came back for a moment. They wanted to cut me out altogether, again.

The customer service officer sensed my emotions, and in a friendly, open manner, he said that since they'd already received an application from me, with a lengthy affidavit stating why I had no access to Jono's death certificate, and numerous supporting documents (he told me he'd actually counted them and told Warren of their vast number), that no, letters of administration for Jono would not overrule my application for Jono's death benefit.

In fact my application may result in me receiving one-hundred per cent of the fund.

They had another few weeks to make an application.

The clock was ticking on my moving-out date. I was going to have to leap before the net was there, and decided I had enough energy to manage one house-hunting day. Annie loaned me her car for the purpose.

There were two rentals in the middle of Pyrmont advertised at what seemed like ridiculously low prices, so I made appointments, hated one and loved the other, applied for it, spent most of my funds on the deposit, and made plans to move.

Claudia and Murray came to help load the truck Jen had, once again, hired. With Jen at the wheel we drove away from the Blue Mountains for the second time in our lives following a significant death, with the dogs up front with us in the cabin.

It felt good to leave the place which was in so many ways a time capsule.

In the sunnier city I pinned my hopes on a new sense of independence and possibility, where I was beholden to no one else in deciding who I had been in Jono's life, and, in ways far more critical, who I was going to be for the rest of mine.

MY house in Pyrmont was sunny and light, built of solid Sydney sandstone a century before, and felt strongly anchored into the very ridge of the suburb, which sits across Darling Harbour from the city proper, connected by Pyrmont Bridge, once a busy vehicle crossing but now set aside for pedestrians.

The house was great apart from the tiny courtyard out the back which was ridiculously small for two energetic Border Collies accustomed to large fenced yards to play in.

But, as Jen pointed out in support of my decision to take this affordable house, when I was not at home they would never be 'doing laps' of any yard, even if it had been an acre of land. They'd be sitting by the door waiting for me to come home. It was also safe for them. No one could get into the backyard, and they couldn't get out.

After living in the Blue Mountains for most of my life, I was prepared for the city to be an extremely unfriendly place for dogs.

My guilt at housing working dogs in that courtyard saw me walk them three times a day — morning, afternoon, and just before bedtime — before they rushed upstairs into their beds on the balcony off my room.

We managed to find every stretch of parkland in the vicinity, and there were plenty more than I first realised, with places for the dogs to get temporarily lost, sniff around bits of scrub and have big runs on the grass.

The first day we found the best way down to the harbour, and, used to regular swimming in the Blue Mountains, Tully took one look at the water and bolted down, leaped over the high sandstone wall, and disappeared.

By the time Olive and I caught up with her, Tully was paddling around having a great time.

Thankfully, the tide had been high and she'd not landed on the oyster-coated rocks piled up against the sea wall, but I started to panic about how I was going to get her out.

It was a silent Sunday morning before any of the locals were up. All that could be heard were the loud glugging noises of Tully's dog paddle.

I looked up and down the harbour wall but there was no jetty or steps. The only possibility that revealed itself was a shipping ladder, far out on a wharf that was blocked by barbed wire.

I tied Olive to a bollard and, full of adrenalin, shimmied my way around the fence and the wire, called Tully across to the ladder, and climbed down, all the while having no concrete plan about how I was going to get her back up.

Without thinking, I grabbed at the thick of her neck, including her collar, with one hand, and, the other on the ladder, in one swift movement, ascended one-handed back to the top.

I then achieved the same kind of circus act holding her out in the air while I swung around the fence and plonked her back on dry land, where she did a very excited dance about the whole thing.

The joy, and the adrenalin, and the ability to save my diminished family from further loss, came together in a moment of sheer survival.

Pyrmont turned out to be full of dogs and extremely dog-friendly people. There was a 'Lassie dog' on a large balcony very high up above street level who would sniff for passing dogs, and we always stopped for her. There was a Pug in a courtyard below street level who would have a friendly bark and a run up and down whenever we passed.

There was a man with a dingo across the street, another little terrier further along, who my girls would visit last thing at night when I let them out the front door to go for a pee on the scrubby median strip of the cul-de-sac's turning circle.

The street had a friendly feel, and all the dogs got on very well.

The Blue Mountains had always been a different matter. Over the years I'd been chased with a stick by an irate dog hater who was convinced Olive was going to attack him, despite her standing about twenty metres away waiting patiently for me to catch up on our walk. There was the old man who laid his boot into her when she was restrained outside the post office, crouching low because she thought his walking stick was part of a game. There was the attack from the Pit Bull Terrier after its lead had not been properly tied to the post, causing injury to me and Olive.

Eventually I'd stopped taking my dogs into public places, where none of the canine residents knew whose territory it was, and the terrible attitude many people exhibited toward others put everyone, animals included, on edge.

In the city everything was more egalitarian.

I would walk the dogs across Darling Harbour, laughing at the way they negotiated the escalators — Tully without a hint of fear, Olive always clutching the ground like it was falling away, but too scared to be left behind. We ventured into Hyde Park, where we'd play a ball game. There was always enough space, even around busy lunch times, and many tourists marvelled at two active Aussie Border Collies who loved to play and pose for photographs.

We found a place at Pyrmont for the dogs to swim in the harbour, down a set of shipping steps where they could leap into the water and swim back with ease. A crowd would always gather at the dogs' antics, fetching the ball and returning it to the top deck.

It was a great way to keep them washed and healthy, since the harbour water had long been cleaner after changes to the collection of pollutants in the major tributaries.

I managed to create a very comfortable home, with most of the furniture Jono and I had collected while we lived together, although I had added to the retro feel of the place with a brilliant original 1970s brown velvet modular lounge purchased from one of the local op shops not long before I left the mountains.

Jono and I had been looking for one for years. On the day he died, I'd seen one abandoned by the side of the road, and had planned to go back and check it out when he got home from work.

On the way back from one of my counselling sessions, many months after that terrible day, something made me go back to the op shop, even though I'd already passed it on my way to the bus stop.

Upstairs, underneath not one but two exercise bikes, was the modular, covered in white flecks, which is why I expected the price had been halved to only sixty dollars.

Ah well, I thought, *it's a shame, because it looks in good condition,* as I brushed at what must have been paint spots.

But they came off! I excavated the modular from its inglorious home, to find its six pieces were in excellent condition, and purchased it on the spot. The softness and comfort of those cushions!

The amazing Fifties lounge had to go. It was unique, but it had never afforded real comfort. I'd put out a call and friends in Lithgow — Sarah and Tim — had taken it off my hands, leaving me with the comfort of brown velvet in Pyrmont, and a lounge I could articulate in a narrow city terrace house by having it wrap around the base of the stairs, creating a safe and cosy nook away from the world.

Thank heaven for the Seventies.

With its vast white walls, the house lent itself to plenty of art, and I snapped up a few Ken Done prints from the 1980s, which, with their incredible colours, lifted the starkness of the place no end. Stacked as they were at the back of op shops, they were cheap as chips.

The ugly wall outside the kitchen window looked brilliant after a coat of paint, a cheap tin of mistint that had been doing nothing at the hardware store.

It was an abundant, safe and colourful home, and the dogs soon took to their courtyard, with a doggy double-bunk made out of plastic bread baskets, cable ties and hessian cushions, sheltered in the cupboard that had been converted from the old outside toilet.

I felt the move had been a good one. By arriving somewhere we'd had our eye on together, part of the story that Jono and I had envisaged was coming true, instead of being ripped away like so much else.

I loved standing on my bedroom balcony at night, listening to the throb of the city, and the distant noises of people, the dogs resting quietly at my feet, watching the world from our eyrie.

Being a cul-de-sac there was very little traffic noise, and everything I needed — shops, movies, life, was at my fingertips if I needed it; but up here, it was distant enough to feel the elemental heart of the ridge beating.

FOURTEEN

WHEN THE CHEQUE finally arrived from Jono's superannuation company I took it to the nearest bank, my heart racing with the fear that somewhere the banking system was going to be alerted to the deposit and something Maureen had engineered would prevent me from being able to access the funds.

But the teller handed me the receipt across the barrier, smiled, and wished me a very nice day, end of story.

The figure at the bottom of the receipt certainly swelled my very diminished funds. I wouldn't have to worry about paying the rent for a while. Not forever, but enough time to get myself mentally and emotionally prepared for work again.

I was finally in the kind of position I'd needed twelve months before: a secure home which I could not be moved on from, with funds to pay for it, and no pressure to work.

How much easier would many, many days in that year have been with that financial support.

I would not have needed to move three times. I would not have been forced to rely on other people to support me in ways which asked them to step right outside their comfort zones. I would not have felt whole weeks of blind panic at the hands of people who were trying to separate me from what was my right as Jono's next-of-kin.

Walking home from the supermarket, past the Sydney Fish Markets, shopping bags in both arms, I pondered whether I might be generous and give Maureen her half of the funds. Jono had, after all, nominated her in addition to me. The thought settled in me, and I mulled it over for the next few days.

Jono and his family often spoke of money. There were some well-embedded family myths about the buying and selling of property which laid a lot of blame at Jono's father's feet for selling a big property in an exclusive suburb in Sydney's Eastern Suburbs in the 1980s and moving north to Bellingen to escape his estranged wife, Maureen, and make a new life for himself.

He'd bought a block of land on a sunny ridge with views from the mountains to the sea, and he'd built himself a blonde brick house with an enormous sun-drenched deck which took in the magnificent views.

A few years later, after the 1990s interest rates crisis, Maureen had sold her flat, followed Joe to Bellingen and bought her own place around the corner.

They never did more than separate. By the time I met them, they lived under a thinly veiled truce, which, as long as he took the blame for selling the family house before the real estate boom, seemed to be fairly affable.

But when alcohol underpinned the conversation, Maureen's bitterness would rise quickly to the surface and spill out all over the place, and if Joe was around, he'd quietly take himself away.

It was always calmer staying with Joe. He and Jono got on very well, and Joe accepted my place in his son's life, ensuring we felt comfortable about sharing the spare room with its double futon, whereas over at Maureen's, we were always left to push two single beds together, beds which seemed willed to stay apart while we were under her roof.

By the time Joe died, Maureen had sold her house after having it on the market for a number of years. She got an excellent Bellingen price for it, and promptly converted the lower ground floor of Joe's house into a flat for herself.

Here she stayed until his death, and, being still married at the time of her estranged husband's demise, she segued neatly into inhabiting his house, and rented out the flat underneath.

Jono flew up to Bellingen to be with his mother and brother when Joe died, and I followed a few days later, not keen on being in the firing line of the family patterns that were so palpable whenever I was around.

Joe's funeral was a simple, heartfelt affair. Both his sons spoke about the man they knew, and it was very fitting.

Nicki, the funeral director, was very helpful with arrangements and seemed to be handling the very difficult situation with great diplomacy.

Jono had mentioned a difficult moment in Nicki's office, when Maureen was becoming upset because Nicki was not looking at her enough. She was technically Joe's widow, after all, if not emotionally.

I remembered further important indicators about family dynamics, six weeks prior to Joe's death.

We all went out to dinner at Bellingen, with Jono's brother Warren and his wife Jane.

It was fairly affable, but Joe was getting very frail and had a bad fall on the kerb while everyone was talking and didn't notice the old man was a bit wobbly, and the weight of the car door saw him slide, knees first, onto the hard concrete gutter, splitting his shin open with copious amounts of blood.

He took it very well when we did our best first aid, stemming the flow of blood enough to see that he was okay and able to be taken home.

But Maureen made an enormous fuss, right out of the blue, seating herself angrily in the passenger seat of one of the cars and flying into a rage.

'He's only bunging it on!' she shouted, folding her arms across her front in the same manner she always did, a pose which seemed to lock her deep within herself.

Warren and Jono both reacted to that, and became two grown men trapped in between their parents, one in genuine need and the other in a fit of jealousy.

We took them home, Jono and I taking Joe up to his room and putting him to bed after cleaning and dressing his wound, while Warren and Jane helped Maureen downstairs.

Much was left unsaid. The next morning, we farewelled them both in the shade of the small courtyard garden by Maureen's front door, wondering what kind of truce, if any, would settle after we'd gone.

Jono never saw his father again.

After the wake, which was held in Joe's living room, Jono and I stayed the night in the spare room, speaking quietly about what was going to happen next. There was a sense of mystery.

The next day dawned with some answers, when Warren arrived and promptly asked for some time with just Jono and his mother.

I got the hint and disappeared into town and waited in one of the cafés. Jono said he'd come and find me when he was ready. We had an afternoon flight back to Sydney, and it was my birthday, so we planned a quiet breakfast before tying things up and heading to the airport.

I had only been waiting a short time when Jono arrived. It seemed as though the family meeting had wrapped up fairly quickly. Jono made a casual mention of the plan that Warren and Maureen had announced about what was going to happen with Joe's house and his estate.

Jono was in a fragile state, so I listened, nodded and understood, in my own way, that he had been told what was happening, not asked.

Back at the house, the architect's plans were out. A giant fortress showed in the artist's impression of what the redeveloped property would look like. Joe's beloved home was to be bulldozed, and replaced by a multi-storey monstrosity.

Maureen seemed focussed, and that was a very good thing. We nodded and encouraged her to do what she needed to do.

Warren drove us to the airport, Maureen in the front seat, me holding Jono's hand in the back. They farewelled us at the gate, and on a brilliant, calm day we flew home.

Neither of them saw Jono ever again.

On the plane, Jono opened up a little about what he'd been told. The house would now go into construction, and Joe's estate would all go into the building of it.

I asked a few questions, but Jono had no answers. All he knew was that he'd been told there was going to be nothing for him.

Because I'd survived the machinations of a sibling intent on manipulating two equally divided estates in my own family, I already knew a bit about how inheritance law worked.

So I tried a few supportive ideas for Jono to take back to Sydney with us, but they fell on deaf ears.

'She's never had anything,' he said of his mother, resigning himself to powerlessness and having his future determined by her, at the age of forty-four. I nodded, not because I agreed, but because I realised it was one of the things Jono often said about his mother.

She might have 'never had anything', but I decided Maureen was not getting half of Jono's superannuation death benefit. She certainly was in no state of financial need.

I remembered the sums of money she had claimed and the struggle I had to maintain my rights at the same time as holding off from strong reactions out of respect for her.

I also realised I had achieved where Jono had failed — I'd managed to extricate myself from a financial relationship with those people.

I finally understood why Jono never made a will in his short life — because he never felt he was independent enough to have anything to leave anyone. A will was simply no use to the man-child his mother had made him.

THE first anniversary of Jono's death came, and Judy, Jen and I went to dinner at the Sydney Dance Company bistro so we could look at his plaque in the corridor.

On the way in we encountered Sam, a former colleague of Judy's and, as it turned out, an old flame of Jono's from two decades before.

The last time I'd seen Sam was at the opening night of one of the shows Jono choreographed, and he'd been there with Amanda. We'd all had a fraught meal together before the show, Jono visibly nervous about the show and his old friends' responses to it.

I was nervous for him, and completely missed the punchline when Sam made an old Sydney joke about us living in 'Far-Kurnell', a reference to what many considered the 'great distance' Kogarah Bay was from the city.

After the show there was little more than ungenerous platitudes from Jono's old friends. It pained him, but he just glossed over it and kept on his path.

Despite his connection to Amanda, the least Sam could do on the night of the first anniversary of Jono's death was show some respect and, to his credit, he did.

Perhaps show-business was less antagonistic towards me now I'd stopped whatever I was 'doing to Jono's mother', or perhaps it wasn't really as shocked as Amanda thought it was? Whatever, I didn't need to be 'nice' to any of them anymore.

Soon after that night, in a cautious manner, Judy said she reckoned she could get me a part-time job with an old contact, Barbara, who worked at the City Recital Hall.

It was day and evening work ushering and staffing the bar and, being a short walk across Darling Harbour, I felt it wouldn't tax me too much, so I rang Barbara, got an interview, and was set to start the next week.

When I arrived for my first shift I realised I was older by many years than most of the staff, apart from a few theatre denizens who seemed well-entrenched in their roles as cloakroom and merchandise sales people. There were the usual unemployed actors and musicians, so I fitted in well enough that I didn't have to reveal the true nature of my current life.

I was assigned to a mobile bar with a young guy who showed me the ropes — we prepared the ice and endless bottles of chilled champagne before being descended on at interval.

Once that short, intense service period was over, a mass washing-up exercise followed with the whole crew clearing the glasses, washing them and wiping them to a perfect polish. It was a great team effort, completed with plenty of camaraderie.

We emptied the bottles into vast recycling bins, so many that we needed padded earphones to protect our ears from the violent noise of glass hitting glass, and were released from our relatively short shift.

The people seemed nice. Nobody asked too many questions. As I made my way home, surrounded by scenes of other venues emptying themselves of rivers of glass bottles after a night of partying in the great boozing city, it felt a cold and isolating place.

In that lonely mood I made my way on foot to a place not far off my route home.

After climbing the staircase and paying my money through a small, lit window, an electronic buzz let me through into a dimly lit locker room, where I found mine using the number on the key I got in exchange for my money.

A few men were milling around, some of them already in their standard issue white towels. I averted my eyes, quickly undressed and put my towel around my naked waist, then walked around the corner following the distant beat of dance music.

The sauna was like every other, plenty of shadows and plenty of levels, cubicle after cubicle of men waiting by doors in split-second appraisal for sexual partners.

I climbed a few floors, afraid to do more than walk, hating the game I was playing to access intimacy.

There were only two options: staying stationary and enduring rejection, or wandering endlessly past cubicles until someone looked twice.

I did the rounds of the top floor, avoiding the light of the high-set television screens which blared pornography that egged us all on to find the same speedy closeness, but no door was opened to me.

As I walked back to the stairwell, a small man passed me and looked wantonly into my eyes, before he swiftly turned and took me through a door with him.

The act, as always, was immediate, a shortcut to passion after anticipation had driven testosterone to the surface of every pore.

He made a few requests of me, which I acquiesced to, even though they were not my preference. Closeness, of any kind, was all I sought that night, because I wouldn't be finding any of it at home.

His pleasure came quickly, I was giving him everything he needed to climb that slope.

I climaxed, and, as I collapsed, part of me wished he would disappear. Another wished he would stay and wrap his arms around me, even though all we lay on was black vinyl, and we'd made whatever love was possible in such an alienating environment.

But he'd gotten what he came for, and he just took himself away.

Heady with emotion, I took myself to the exposed showers and washed the day away, hurriedly dressed and was back on the pathway home before I realised that in my rush to find elusive intimacy, I had used absolutely no protection.

That decision, or the lack of one, came to haunt me for months.

Although I was living permanently in the city, once a month I caught the train up to the Blue Mountains to see Michael, my counsellor, where the story of that night was retold.

I saw him bristle for a moment, then he validated my need for intimacy, or 'oblivion' as he called it, on a night when I was right out of my comfort zone: starting a new job, meeting new people, and having to cope with it all without my life partner. Then he recommended I have an HIV test.

He came with me the next morning, and we sat on the grass across the road from the clinic in the gardens of the hospital where my mother had worked for ten years.

The sense of my long-dead mother was palpable in that place. Michael had known and worked with her, and the concern on his face told me that I had walked in territory that was all too familiar to him, a grief counsellor who had worked at the peak of the HIV-AIDS pandemic.

Sometimes I would ask Michael about those times, because I realised how close my current widowed situation was to many relationships he had witnessed, made worse by a total lack of relationship recognition for men whose partners came out to their relatives, just before telling them they were terminally ill. The echoes of that time sat in Michael's responses, and it pulled me up short. My carelessness was reprehensible as much as it was understandable.

I would have to wait a week for the test results, and have another test in a further three months, during which I might seroconvert and acquire the HIV virus, irreversibly.

Seroconversion is different for all HIV cases — some people experience virus-like symptoms, a rash, a sore throat, aching joints or similar maladies; some people experience nothing; and some experience an extended illness.

I was prepared for anything, and yet I was prepared for absolutely nothing at all, and entered a work-life stasis in order to get through.

Had a brief sexual encounter drawn me back to a pathway which may lead to an untimely death, or would I be spared?

I'D leased a two-bedroom house with a plan to eventually rent the second to a flatmate when I was ready, and when the time came I placed an ad on a gay-friendly accommodation website. There were two responses, and both seemed very keen on taking the room.

The first was an athletic guy who rode a bike he'd need accommodated in the tiny courtyard. When I asked him a bit about himself he said he'd email me a link, which I thought was a bit strange, but I just nodded and said okay.

When it came, I got my first taste of online gay hook up sites, with more of my potential flatmate revealed than I was prepared for. I didn't respond, and never heard from him again.

The second was a rather lonely fellow with an unusual name he admitted he'd made up for himself.

He came around to look at the place late one evening, and settled himself into the velvet lounge in a very suggestive manner, before revealing that he had what he called 'the plague'.

I swallowed and probably blinked, reminded of my own waiting game around the same disease, and said it didn't matter. At that, he assumed I was also HIV positive, which seemed to delight him in a manner that told me he expected more from me than just a flatmate arrangement.

I lied that there were others interested, and a week later emailed to say the room had gone to someone else.

The idea of saunas terrified me now that I had not only possibly exposed myself to HIV, with a case of crabs to boot, so I had a look at the online dating sites, and thought perhaps I could find some form of intimacy there, without the fraught emotions and danger.

The application forms were long-winded, seeking all kinds of information, most of which I was unwilling to give. The gay community wanted all the obvious specifics. I was not prepared to define myself in that way, so I shut the computer down.

At work, there was a wonderful coterie of gay men — actors, musicians and writers. One of them — Adam — I found myself drawn to. We got on well and had a good time, mucking around like men a lot younger.

I tried to get to know him, and let him know me, by sharing bits and pieces of my story with him. One night after work, we went for a drink with a couple of others, and stayed talking for a while, before saying goodnight.

I felt open to Adam, but wasn't sure how he felt about me, so I just left things alone.

In the meantime, my flatmate issue sorted itself when Annie announced she needed a place to live for a few months while she went through the motions of buying a flat just across the city.

It was perfect, since we had ostensibly lived together already, she knew my state of affairs, and she knew my dogs and they loved her.

One Saturday night, Annie told me she planned to bring a date home. I decided to give them some space by meeting Adam up at Darlinghurst, and walked the whole way to where he'd made a loose arrangement to meet me. Crossing Hyde Park, I decided that I'd make a move that night. A desire for intimacy and validation possessed me.

The hill of Oxford Street loomed brightly with all its lights on show, and my determination increased as I ascended, eschewing all the promises of the sauna stairs at street level for the promise of a drink with someone nice, ideally more.

When I got to the bar, I wasn't able to see Adam until I was practically on top of him in the throng, but it became quickly apparent that Adam and a new friend were already fixed up for the night.

I played it cool when we were introduced: a doctor, from somewhere in Europe. Nice looking. Adam was infatuated.

I must have looked terribly crestfallen, because when his lover excused himself and went to the bathroom, Adam said: 'This is so frustrating, this kind of thing never happens to me, two men interested in me on the same night!'

I needed to get out of there, made some lame excuse about meeting other friends somewhere, which Adam had the empathy to accept without question, and I went my way.

My devastated feet found their way to the same sauna, the same stairwell, key and towel. I took to a cubicle this time, and waited, figuring I'd had enough bad luck already.

It's a risk, being the one in the cubicle, who must accept or reject those who cross the threshold. I was approached by a man who matched none of what I seek sexually, but there was something about him which allowed me to close the door. This time I embarked on safe sex.

It was very late. Perhaps he noticed something in me which kept him from fleeing seconds after orgasm, when he put an arm around me, and, with a lovely singing voice, started to join the speakers on that floor in a rendition of 'Separate Lives'.

My emotions brimmed over, and I told him about my life at that time. He listened, but remained remote, then asked outright if he could stay the night, since he'd missed the last train to Wollongong.

I didn't want to go home alone, so I agreed. We went through the motions of leaving the sauna together, crossed Darling Harbour in the very early light, and fell into bed.

He held me, and I found myself responding, although in my heart I knew it was as though he was Jono, taking the practiced pathway that we knew provided the other with the greatest pleasure.

In that way I got a version of what I needed, but I was fooling myself as part of the bargain.

FIFTEEN

LISA LEFT A message on my mobile phone in which she simply said: 'If you can forgive me, please give me a call.'

At the sound of her voice, something in me opened and I rang immediately. I was a little wary, because Lisa had first met Jono in Bellingen and she knew Maureen quite well. I didn't want any doors opening to that energy, so I agreed to meet Lisa on neutral ground to see where the land lay.

She had finished her course in Canberra and was now living in Sydney, working as a freelance designer.

'I just needed to do some growing up,' she said, the distance from the acute grief of losing one of her closest friends giving both of us some perspective.

We slipped back into our friendship on healed terms. She was honest enough to tell me she had contacted Maureen, and why: because she'd needed to talk with someone who'd known Jono.

But I knew I would have to take Lisa back into my life on faith alone, and allow her the space to show me some new actions, while forgiving her for those which had hurt me.

That would need time.

We started by going to the beach with the dogs. Lisa would call me in the afternoon and turn up with her car and we'd all pile in and head for the Eastern Suburbs to a place where we could always get a car park and wander down to McKenzie's Rocks, north of Tamarama and south of Bondi.

Over the years, people had made a path down to the ocean

between large rocks, away from the main beaches, and nobody freaked out if you had a dog with you.

Olive and Tully thought it was a great adventure, and they took to the water as willingly as Lisa and I. This wasn't a conventional beach experience with a sandy strand, it was channels of white water crossing the rock shelves, leaving little pools, as turbulent as spas.

Here, in the noise and constant wash of the sea, Lisa and I had all our rough edges gently tumbled away by the force of nature. We played, like children, in a manner that comes easily to Lisa, and which she taught me by example with a generous spirit.

Each time we got a little braver, and we'd challenge one another into deeper dives into channels further out, where swimmers could get washed into the ocean and have to find their way back around to the beach to avoid dangerous rocks.

When the returning waves pulled us, they pulled hard, and our giggling turned to gurgles in those moments when the salt and water and sand caught us in a whirlpool, tumbling us over one another in a mix of delight and terror.

Once, Lisa was taken off guard and swept below the surface of one large channel, me on the ocean side. I could see she might be in trouble, so I stuck my arm under the water, clamped onto a limb as she was swept past, and pulled her back into the air with an assertive force.

We inhaled, acknowledging that life is brittle and fun can turn into terror, then we both dived in again.

In the whole process of my grief, those swimming games at McKenzie's Rocks, the dogs happily amusing themselves sniffing after crabs and fetching sticks in gentle ponds of healing water, with two inner children, me and Lisa, cavorting with no deadline, no one we needed to tell where we were, were some of the most healing times for me.

They restored my faith in friendship, and they went a very long way in restoring my faith in life, not just living it, but participating in it, despite all the obvious danger.

I CAN'T remember the name of that sympathetic guy I took home to my bed, even though it turned out he was the former boyfriend of someone I worked with, an irony he never felt comfortable with, because it was obvious he was still very much in love with my colleague.

It was odd, being a rebound man for one of my rebound men. He seemed keen for me to catch the train to his home in the Illawarra, even met me at the station, then walked awkwardly at my side to his house before lightening up, in private, in a manner I knew all too well, because I did it myself. It was a sizing up, a trying on.

Are you the one? We silently asked, even though we knew we were not.

I spent a trashy weekend in his flat, the only trashy weekend I have ever had in my life. I was not drunk, or drugged, I was only subdued by a desperation to make something work.

For this man, I thought, *I will give up my sexual need. I will reinvent myself into something he needs.*

Having experienced great loss, I was trying to experience some kind of win, and I was prepared to change myself to do it. Others seemed to be able to achieve it.

I tried my level best all weekend to bed this needy man, and when he relinquished, his flatmate arrived home and promptly went to the balcony, where he copped a full view of us. The intimacy was cut with the sudden shutting of the blind.

The morning came with the terrible knowledge that this man wanted me gone, yet I would not go, could not go. I was in the middle of a failed reinvention and I didn't want my experiment so suddenly cancelled.

He tried to shirk me all day, as we ate and watched a movie neither of us enjoyed.

That night, I sank into a silent despair, crying with a face so still I might have been dead, the sense of the ocean, just by the terrible flat, reminded me of a wide world that cared not one shred about me, about us, about this terrible dance of shame.

He had to work in the morning and left me alone in his empty flat, a place of compromise, his lonely post-relationship world, into which I had escaped from mine.

It was not only death which could bring such separation, but being left, left to our own devices.

I MADE the appointment for my three-month HIV test a week before it was due, at the sexual health clinic at Katoomba, and duly caught my train from Sydney's central railway, a journey I had taken hundreds of times in the three decades I lived in the Blue Mountains.

As the train shunts its way through Redfern, and multiple track changes before Strathfield, I always found time to think and reflect, to ruminate on whatever experience the city had delivered to me that day: theatre productions, shopping sprees, whatever.

But after leaving Strathfield, it picks up speed and hurtles its way to Parramatta, and sleep is possible if you let go.

That day, I couldn't let go. About a fortnight before I'd had an exhausting week, seemingly for no reason, a niggling sore throat and flu-like symptoms.

I couldn't tell anyone. I could hardly tell myself, let alone begin the journey to acceptance that I may have seroconverted in that window of time the HIV virus has to settle into the human body.

Once, half asleep on a ferry to Watson's Bay with Judy, on our way to meet Jen, who was house sitting for her boss, I let Judy know what my fear was about all this exhaustion.

She did not flinch, which I took as a kind of acceptance, of me, and of the reality that was unfolding.

So, approaching the clinic, I needed more help. I asked Claudia to come with me.

In the darkness of the waiting room, we joked about the brochures, all the sexually transmitted diseases from A to Z. Claudia and I laughed indulgently.

We always did, she and I, chortling and guffawing deeply to fill the voids of life with humour, because there always seemed to be bad news waiting just around the corner.

The echoes of our laughing died away, when I noticed the receptionist was still speaking with the nurse, murmuring coming through the waiting room window, which gave onto an old enclosed verandah connecting the clinic rooms enough to hear that something was being communicated, something important.

I gulped and looked down. The nurse's footsteps approached, and we were taken into her room and seated, my anonymous file placed in front of her.

I'd lived with that file for a relatively short period of time, since I had come out and become a sexually active gay man. Filled with negative results for tests like oral gonorrhea, syphilis, information on hepatitis inoculations and all the standard tests, Jo, the clinic nurse, always made the same joke at this moment: that I was so boring and must have a terrible sex life, to be filling her files with all these negative results.

I gave a half laugh, expecting no punchline, when she said today was no different. My second HIV test had come back negative.

In the relief of more laughter and exhalation, of calling my sister with the good news and going for lunch in Katoomba, I floated along just above the surface of the great truth: I had escaped the gateway to death again, and I should not tempt its proximity again.

HAVING been politicised by the 2004 federal election, my media radar for marriage equality began to function, and I became a regular reader of the news pages in Sydney's gay media.

After John Howard and Phillip Ruddock's work on amending the Marriage Act, that media was filled with the very early work of the grassroots movement which evolved into the national campaign for marriage equality.

I took myself to political meetings, for the Gay and Lesbian

Rights lobby, and others, but found little solace. My story held very little currency in the gay community.

One guy at a lobby meeting spoke passionately about the lack of gay rights before the NSW de-facto laws were amended to include same-sex couples in 1999, another reminder of how the HIV-AIDS pandemic had cut through relationships and human rights.

There had been shocking scenes in the hospital system, where understanding was either given or denied, with very little of the middle ground which might have supported families had there been decent legislation to ensure surviving spouses were not cut out of estates.

Very often, surviving spouses didn't outlive their deceased partners long enough to work anything out.

There was a great *'what would be the use of it?'* question hanging over the early days of the marriage equality movement in Australia.

A gay community tentatively coming to terms with the survival rates of combination anti-retroviral therapies seemed too exhausted to fight for marriage equality.

The 1999 NSW legislation was hard fought enough for some, and they let it be known they were tired and just needed time to work out if they were going to survive.

The story of my banishment from Jono's death certificate had few precedents, but it had happened, and some men I encountered told me the legal ways to avoid it happening, which was no use now that it had happened.

HIV-AIDS was such an enormous presence in the gay community that the death of a gay man could hardly be described without reference to it. Many assumed that's what had killed Jono.

When I went to a gay bookshop to find a non-fiction book about gay grief, there was nothing, and the shop assistant suggested I try Timothy Conigrave's account of the death of his partner in *Holding the Man*. HIV-AIDS, again.

I wrote a few letters to the editor of the Sydney gay weeklies, and got challenged by other readers for creating a problem where they saw there was none.

A journalist eventually contacted me and asked if I'd like to give an interview about the experience of losing Jono. I agreed, and we met at Hyde Park while he recorded me explaining what had occurred.

He was very young, a fact which probably led me to over explain my story, but also led me to a realisation.

It was so simple, really. This was not a gay thing, this problem of trying to find context and understanding in my story, it was just that few people wanted to talk about death. Talking about it would lead to thinking about it, and the sudden, unexplained death of a forty-four-year-old man was all the more confronting.

The piece was published a few weeks later. Adam, my colleague at the recital hall, told me he thought I could have done better writing it myself, and I knew he was right.

I had offered my story to someone so inexperienced that the finer political points of a same-sex spouse's death were not communicated.

I came across as a fish out of water, which I suppose I was, yet the trashing of human rights around same-sex relationships was still invisible in my country.

CLAUDIA and Murray got married later that year.

They'd been together for five years, had a child, and blended their families when Murray's kids moved in at different times. Everyone who knew them was delighted at this turn of events.

I was very happy for them, and gladly volunteered my time for the event by writing out the place cards for the reception.

Claudia asked me to speak, and I agreed without thinking. As the big day approached, I got more and more upset about this task. What did I have to say about a relationship? What did I have to say about marriage? What did I have to say about our friendship, in the light of what had happened between me and many of my friends since Jono's death?

I put myself in the moment and imagined it to be quite horrific and a little unfair of her, so I asked her if she'd like to find someone else, perhaps someone in her family.

Claudia's response came swiftly: 'Do you even want to come?' she said.

I was taken aback, apologised profusely, and got to planning what I would say.

A week later, surrounded by their loved ones, including their children, Claudia and Murray were married at a beautiful ceremony.

The time came for my speech. I spoke about my friend and her journey to this moment, keeping it light, and did my level best to bless their relationship from the perspective of someone whose life partner had died fifteen months before, and encouraged them not to fear the worst.

In the pub across the road afterwards, Claudia's brother Mac told me he felt for me. When I asked him why, he acknowledged that speaking for 'the happy couple' must have been very hard.

Claudia came up to us, and Mac made a point of remembering that I'd taken his sister into my home when she'd needed one after rehab. I tried to brush him off, diplomatically, but he was having none of it.

'When you needed her help, she threw you out!' he said, putting an arm around his sister.

Her bridal glow was strong, and I wasn't about to be blamed for its tarnishing, so I said: 'Remember, Mac, I left Claudia and Murray's place. They didn't throw me out.'

It was enough to end that thread of conversation, but not enough to change the truth.

I MET Steve at a beat. The first thing I noticed about him were his eyes: deep pools, darker than the darkness that enveloped us.

He must have noticed something in me, because we swapped numbers, and went our ways.

Only a few hours later I arrived at his door. We spoke for a few minutes, taking in the way we both really looked. Like me, he'd worn a baseball cap to hide his baldness, and indeed, it had taken years off him.

But in the light he was no less beautiful. Those eyes were framed by long lashes, and again, they were the deepest thing in the room.

I prattled, as I always did in such situations, then allowed myself to be made love to for the first time since being in Jono's arms.

I almost stayed the night, but I thought of the dogs on their little balcony, and tore myself away from his bed in the early morning.

Steve wanted to date. We went to the beach, we went out for dinner, we spoke of our lives. We were mature enough and comfortable enough to speak about our disappointments. I told him about Jono, that I felt like used goods, but he didn't seem to care.

In the middle of all this romance, I needed to go into hospital for a small operation. Steve deftly handled my patched up body, working around the dressing with a loving skill.

But we were doomed.

Something was missing. We'd taken a shortcut to a relationship. If we'd met at a party, had not already dived so deeply into one another, perhaps we'd have had a chance.

When our faces met, as they always did in our lovemaking, there was a shadow of shame between us, like we were both about to burst out laughing and shout that it's impossible to build a relationship on what we were doing.

I cared about Steve. I have only ever written one 'Dear John' letter, and that was to him, because he loved me well enough to heal something in me, to make me feel lovable and attractive, despite no longer owning the blossom of youth so desperately desired by many in the gay community.

GABRIELLA and Dan were also married not long before the year came to an end. Annie had raised Dan as an integral part of her family, and was therefore very involved in the preparations. Gabriella and I had worked together, and she very generously invited me too.

On the day, Annie and I were tasked with collecting the wedding cake before heading over to Watson's Bay for the ceremony.

At the bakery, Annie quite naturally asked for the 'Gabriella-Dan wedding cake', which seemed to confuse the manager, who disappeared for a minute and came back looking very annoyed.

'They didn't tell me it was for a wedding,' she grumbled as she handed it over.

Under the thrall of hair and make-up at the Watson's Bay Hotel, Gab laughed and explained how she'd avoided being ripped off by telling the bakery the cake was for her brother's homecoming celebration, not for a wedding!

It was very moving to witness Gabriella and Dan's families bless their union in many very special ways, particularly Gabriella's father, who paid tribute to his daughter in a manner so touching and supportive it struck me to the core.

Afterwards, I skirted the crowded dance floor, feeling a bit out of place.

The night, the setting, the sight of beautiful people deeply in love within loving families, seemingly immune to the kind of disenfranchisement I had been a victim of, was almost overwhelmingly bittersweet.

TOWARDS the end of my second year without Jono I started to wake up.

I don't know if it was a side effect of grief, but gradually a woolly layer started to fall away from around me. I'd handled two weddings, and started saying yes to invitations from friends to go to the movies, parties and other gatherings.

It left me exhausted, but I felt okay as long as I knew I could get home and put my feet up.

The numbness had seen me switch off to the news of the day. I paid little attention to media content, including major stories such as Schapelle Corby's arrest and subsequent trial, and the news at Christmas 2004, when a quarter of a million people were wiped out in the Boxing Day Tsunami.

I knew it had happened, of course, but I did not take it in. One death, to me, was more than enough to be dealing with at that time.

Eventually the blanket lifted, and I started a process of emergence. I managed to join the family Christmas at Woy Woy Bay, armed with a few strategies for self care and avoiding doing too much, and attended a New Year celebration at Sarah and Tim's place at Lithgow on one of the hottest summer nights on record.

I slept the night on the Fifties divan Jono and I had purchased at an op shop all those years before. Sarah and Tim had taken the whole suite off my hands, and they had it nestled in their lovely rambling house in the bush.

Olive and Tully slept at my feet. Naumi eventually came in and took the other side of the divan, and we got to giggling like we were kids. Sarah noticed as she passed in the half light, and remarked on it.

I was laughing. I was laughing like a little child, Jono's presence underneath me, chatting into the hot summer night at the beginning of another year, and I wasn't pretending.

SIXTEEN

AFTER CLAUDIA MANIFESTED a job as a magazine feature writer and editor, she rang me a few times in a state of panic, harried by having to interpret copy-editing terms.

I was very glad to give her an understanding ear and helped by googling terminology for her while she was on the other end of the phone. It was another sign I was a little bit more capable, a little more recovered.

She started sending me suitable job ads, and I duly applied. Working at the recital hall was fun, but it also felt like a backward career step.

Part of me really didn't know if I could ever make it as an actor. I loved the work, but the networking required to get employment seemed totally impossible to manifest without a decent agent, and all my attempts to get a connected agent came to nothing.

There were jobs within the Sydney gay print media, and after the experience of being the subject of an interview — not a particularly good one — I decided to try my hand at those. Immediately, I got a couple of interviews.

I turned up at the specified time and was met by very young, very cool gay men, who whisked me into a shared office for a sub-editing test, leaving me to interpret that if I passed that, I might get an interview.

The first time I failed miserably, or was left to assume I had, since when I took so long on the one-page dummy article that nobody bothered to come and check if I had completed it. When I went to hand it in, everyone was at lunch, so I left it with the receptionist and disappeared.

I was better prepared at my next chance, managing to sub the copy fairly quickly and accurately, and got to meet one of the editors across a desk where he asked me for a series of article ideas.

Every one of mine saw him roll his eyes and look out the window, saying: 'Yes … we've already done that,' impatiently.

I had nothing to lose, so I waited until he looked me in the eye, and I said: 'Well, they're obviously good ideas if you've already done them,' at which he was so confronted he showed me out.

I started to look at online job networks, and soon found something that was more up my alley, in fact it was almost line for line the job description of the last contract I'd had in the United Kingdom.

It was a position I waited many years to find which saw me producing documentaries across Britain and North America, a role I loved and thought I'd be able to replicate soon after arriving back home in Australia.

Here, after eight years of career struggle, was essentially the same job, so I applied with great enthusiasm, putting aside the full-time nature of the work so that I didn't lose my steam.

I got an interview and found the company a friendly, small crew. My referees in the United Kingdom happened to be in the same office when the company's managing director called them. More serendipity.

And then the offer, at which I gushed with relief, explaining that when the boss knew me a little better, he would understand what good fortune it all was.

THAT week, I got a call out of the blue from the young journalist who'd interviewed me. He'd been contacted by a guy called Walter who wanted to get in touch with me about the article.

I agreed to give Walter my email address, and a few days later he contacted me, writing how good the news was about the changes to the rules at the NSW Registry of Births, Deaths and Marriages, and that by now I must be celebrating about getting hold of Jono's death certificate.

Reading those words filled me with energy, but it was a jaded force. My experience had led me to plenty of blind alleys and awkward folk who professed help but actually revealed hindrances. Perhaps this Walter would be the same?

I responded rather casually that I had not heard any news about changes to the Registry's practices.

Walter replied almost immediately, letting me know that he worked within the Registry and had been party to the rule changes being discussed quite recently. He expressed confidence that I would be able to make a successful application for Jono's death certificate independently.

It was so long since I had any hope on that front that I didn't immediately know what to do, so I called the Registry, managed to fob off the customer service staff, got put through to a manager, and made an appointment to meet him the next day.

He said I would need evidence to back up my claim for access.

I had only to reach for the bulging file by my bed, full of statutory declarations, statements, my affidavit, and almost seventy forms of documentation that warranted the existence of my relationship with Jono.

The first thing that shocked me about the NSW Registry of Births, Deaths and Marriages was the level of security. Bouncers, thick glass screens, metal-detecting barriers, and an air of protection pervaded the place.

That's when I realised why I'd had such a tough time with this institution: they control access to some of the most important life decisions we enter into as citizens, so they expect problems and they're in a permanent state of lockdown.

Upstairs, the manager invited me to show him the documentation in my possession. His eyes widened, and he went to stand, saying he only needed to photocopy the first three.

But I couldn't let him go. I got extremely angry and emotional at having to wait for this moment much longer than a straight spouse in my position would have had to. In the nineteen months prior I'd been brought to my knees emotionally and financially.

I'd survived suicidal thoughts, processed deep shame, lost friends, and had to move far too often because I'd been forced to become a ball of unmanageable humanity by the shortcomings of one family and the internal regulations of this man's department.

He was not getting away with just copying a few documents.

I already sensed he was trapped between his feelings of homophobia and the new guidelines which now required him to treat me equally, a full seven years after the NSW laws had changed.

He managed to squeeze out that he reckoned I had a very good case, and that if a new certificate were to be issued, all the old copies would be recalled for destruction.

Did he need the details of exactly where those fraudulent copies were now?

'Yes,' he mumbled, shamefaced.

I handed over the names and addresses for him to request the return of the death certificate which had been created for me, long withheld by the funeral director I'd contracted and held in their safe behind a wall of defensiveness and avoidance; and the other at Jono's family's disposal, already widely distributed to claim that I, Jono's surviving spouse, did not exist.

At that, he looked as though he'd shit his pants.

A WEEK later, Naumi, Sarah and I treated ourselves to yum cha and Sydney's first screening of *Brokeback Mountain*.

This story of two men who could barely come out to one another, let alone live as a couple the way Jono and I had, saw me stumble into a cubicle in the bathroom as soon as it finished.

I could barely breathe. All I could do was lean against the wall, my legs buckling under me, some unseen force creeping up them and into my trunk.

It was the shirts Ennis del Mar discovered in the dead Jack Twist's boyhood bedroom, Ennis' inside Jack's, as simple and as primal an expression of love as they come.

I still had one of Jono's shirts, retrieved from the dirty clothes basket after his death, full of his scent. I had buried my head in its folds so often that it became a guilty pleasure.

Had taking that shirt into the manager's office at the Registry of Births, Deaths and Marriages in Sydney stood to make a difference, I would have done it.

I composed myself. The country was about to experience the

doomed 'gay cowboy' love story of Ennis and Jack up on the big screen, and yet the two men were not gay, not in the true sense.

As much as they may have wanted to cohabit, Ennis and Jack had not reached that stage of finding the myriad of reasons to stay together, all the joyous ones in addition to the few painful and confronting.

In some ways, *Brokeback Mountain* seemed to me an offensive fantasy. One critic rightly suggested that a man like Ennis del Mar, around the age of forty in the early 1980s, could have found his way from Wyoming to San Francisco and found love again.

But the world still needed unhappy endings for gay cowboys.

I walked with Naumi and Sarah to Chinatown, then crept home across Darling Harbour. In the letterbox, a plain envelope had come from the Registry, inviting me to collect Jono's death certificate whenever I was ready.

I could have gotten it from the front desk, but I booked an appointment with the manager and I made him give it to me, right into my hand.

There, on the same document, was Jono's name and mine, his marital status listed as 'De-Facto', a record of the exact number of years we had been together, and his occupation listed as Producer: the truth which had frightened the homophobes in our lives finally laid bare in paper form as indelible as any gravestone. I cried a little, and then I went downstairs to apply for another original.

The young woman took the form and immediately shook her head, tapped her finger on my name and Jono's, and said: 'You can't get this, not when you're the same gender.'

I was not surprised. I said to her, calmly so as not to set off any security screens or draw the attention of the bouncers, that she was incorrect and needed to ask her manager for some training on this issue. The jaw, that had been munching so enthusiastically on chewing gum, went motionless.

I went upstairs and saw the manager's distorted face through the glass as I made the same demand of him and his colleagues. Not one of them would come out of their office to meet me.

Lisa took my photo out the front. In the sunlight, the white blaze of the important document in my hand showed like a victory flag.

When I recall that day, it comes with a sense that I had started to dry out from the inside, like a sickness leaving my body.

I WAS keen to set the record straight with all the players in this drama that had separated me from Jono's death certificate, so I embarked on the creation of a letter which explained the outcome.

I still have a copy of this never-sent letter, in which I coldly outlined the truth.

When I showed Lisa, she recognised I was dealing with the latest round of pain. Perhaps she also recognised the fear it would cause Maureen to see that her web of denial had been broken.

Almost against my will, Lisa guided my hand to do something which I had not planned, as I took a match to the photocopy of Jono's falsified death certificate on which my name never appeared, and had been waved under my nose to mollify me when legal shenanigans were underway.

We stood in the tiny courtyard of the house at Pyrmont as that shitty piece of paper became ash before my eyes, and I said, out loud, that I need not write to Maureen and Warren, or the funeral director Luke, or his boss, Wayne, who'd told me to 'do my worst' to get my copy of Jono's death certificate out of his safe.

I had what I needed. That had to be enough.

But I felt like a child, shamed into submission, when all I wanted to do was strike back, to inflict pain, in answer to the pain that had been inflicted on me.

So I wrote to NSW's highest legal advocate, Attorney-General Bob Debus, and made him aware of my case, suggesting some kind of public awareness campaign and staff training were urgently needed to ensure same-sex couples in his jurisdiction knew their rights and Registry customer service officers acted according to the law.

When I didn't receive a reply, I turned to one of NSW's greatest shit-kickers for the LGBTIQA+ community, then independent Member for Bligh and Sydney's Lord Mayor Clover Moore. A councillor in one of the world's great gay cities, she understood the issue immediately, and wrote to speed a response from Mr Debus.

We never received more than a courteous staffer's assurance that the matter was being looked into.

SOON after, I dreamed of Jono again.

I was home at Pyrmont, a house he and I never shared, on a sunny day that sent shafts of light through the front window, and Jono let himself in.

We greeted one another. I was desperate to kiss him and hold him, but all he wanted to do was go upstairs and unpack his things in the bedroom, my bedroom, where we never slept together and the only piece of his clothing was the one shirt I had kept from the dirty clothes basket.

He started to explain where he'd been — stuck in transit. I accepted his story without rancour, and as he piled his clothes back with mine on the shelves and I lay on the bed overjoyed to see him, I said to him in a strong, clear, low voice: 'Okay, I have something to tell you about your family.'

He stopped piling his clothes onto mine, and started to turn to me, but before I could see his face and interpret the still, pained angle of his shoulders, I woke up.

I TOOK to my new job with as much energy as I could muster, participating in the production of television commercials and corporate videos. Luckily it was a no-nonsense company, and I was given plenty of space to grow into the role.

The commute across the Sydney Harbour Bridge by train to St Leonards saw me having to fight my way into my local station — Town Hall — against the tide of city workers that poured out and down to Darling Harbour. On the way home the tide went in reverse.

I walked the dogs first thing every weekday, and as soon as I got home we piled out the door and belted around the Pyrmont peninsula for another round of exercise.

All the guilt of having them cooped up in a tiny courtyard all day diminished, along with more of my waistline.

On an average day, I ascended and descended thousands of

steps, the last of which were the steep stairs up to my bedroom, where I collapsed for the night, and often thought of Annie — now moved out to her city flat — and how she would often laugh about climbing those last steps on hands and knees, especially at the end of the day.

Sometimes I woke in the night to the barest sounds of lovemaking through the wall. A couple on one side seemed to prefer midnight sex. The woman on the other side appeared to be single, but sometimes, on a weekend, she got lucky.

Across the road, public housing units were filled with an array of lives coming and going at all hours.

Me and the dogs made a few friends, other dog owners, usually. The third walk of every day, just before bed, saw us pass and say goodnight to Gizmo and his owner, a lonely looking man who'd say, wistfully, every time: 'Have a nice night,' before disappearing into the shadows of his carport.

Olive and Tully watched the denizens of the night from their balcony. Trained never to bark, they softly grizzled and whimpered if a friendly dog passed, usually Lestat, the enormous male Rottweiler who exuded a scent which drove my girls into fits of very quiet, very sweet, passion.

I'd lie in the shafts of light, reminiscent of moonlight but only the last vestiges of light from the neon signs at the top of the Sydney casino, I still missed Jono terribly and wondered what happened to my life, that surely this shock was someone else's to bear, and not mine.

I FINALLY got to meet Walter, the man who helped me access Jono's death certificate after he'd contacted me about the interview I'd given to the gay media.

Lisa and some friends from the recital hall had planned a picnic at the annual Sydney Gay and Lesbian Mardi Gras Fair Day at Victoria Park, and I asked Walter to meet me at the entrance to the swimming pool, right in the thick of the event.

Fair Day was pumping as usual, but Lisa and the others were waiting for us in the shade at the edge of the throng, where you could hear yourself talk.

It was a glorious, relaxing afternoon with new friends, an old friend, and the man who'd found the link to Jono I'd sorely needed.

Adam was still at the edge of my consciousness. Someone was taking photos, and I was pleased when I handed one of the dogs to Adam and he scooped her up enthusiastically into his arms.

We all smiled as the moment was captured, a moment that seemed full of potential.

SEVENTEEN

THE STORY OF Jono's death made its way through the entertainment industry like an urban myth, meaning I sometimes had to deal with distant friends who were only just catching up with events more than a year after the fact.

This semi-resolved state I was in led me to look up Jono's ex-partner David, who I tracked down though the AIDS Council of NSW where he was an employee.

I emailed him to ensure that he heard about Jono's death from someone caring. He replied that he did not know, and thanked me for telling him.

Jono had often spoken about his relationship with David, the only other significant partnership in his life, and the pain of their separation. That had driven him up to Bellingen in the first place, seeking a sense of place after the devastation of being left.

I felt no ill will towards David, in fact, I began to feel the exact opposite. Here was another man who had loved and been loved by Jono. We were Team Jono.

Eventually, I shared a little of my experience of Jono's mother and brother with David, and he gently confirmed that his experience of Maureen and Warren had been similar.

That made me feel considerably better, to know that this experience would have been the same for any man who had been Jono's partner at the time of his death.

David told me he visited a special place they'd had, to say his goodbye to Jono in his own way.

Despite his mother and brother's lack of interest in Jono as a self-determined homosexual man, he'd had two significant relationships with loving men in the same short lifetime. What a victory for him.

NOT long after Annie moved out, Claudia's husband Murray asked if he could stay in my spare room for a few nights in order to attend a building certification course in the city.

I said yes immediately, knowing what commuting to and from the city had become for Blue Mountains residents. The dogs, particularly Olive, loved Murray.

I could still recall returning home to the presence, the scent, of another man in the house.

It was a moment of sadness for me, but also realisation. The day Jono and I decided we'd move in together came with an expression of our desire to live as a family, not with flatmates. Like just about everyone we knew, we'd grown tired of the whole flatmate thing.

I remember when Claudia and Murray reached the same point in their relationship, it was that energy which drove Murray to build them all an enormous home, perhaps his life's work.

Having this solid family man around my home for two nights was a reminder of the power of choosing to live as a family, and I knew in my heart that I could not live the rest of my life without it.

Claudia came to the city on the last afternoon of Murray's course — she'd won tickets to an event at Darling Harbour. Murray and I got home from walking the dogs, just as Claudia arrived.

While he got his things, Claudia and I caught up. She confessed how Murray had felt a bit awkward about asking me if he could stay, considering the way things had gone when I last stayed with them.

I laughed it off, not wanting to revisit the pain, but I also thought it was a good thing their choices had come back to haunt them, even just a little.

A few weeks later, Claudia called me on my mobile phone at work during the morning. Little Sam was in hospital after a night of respiratory problems, Claudia was tired and emotional. Because Murray was at work he could not mollify her concerns at that moment.

I talked her through it, and encouraged her to understand that Sam was okay, he was in the right place, and, in just a few hours, Murray would be able to visit his little boy in the hospital. Perhaps he'd be allowed to go home by then? That seemed to help, and Claudia rang off.

The next day, she rang me at home, apologised for calling me at work, and said that Sam was fine and home from hospital. I told her that she didn't need to be sorry, she could call me anytime, my boss was not the kind of man who would get upset about friends in need.

But Claudia persisted in her line of apology. It was beyond sorry, it was something else, like she was testing how much impact she'd had on my day.

'It's okay, you're not that powerful,' I said, and laughed.

'What am I supposed to say to that?' she asked, delicately breaking before hanging up.

I called back but she wouldn't answer. I left a message, trying to explain that what I'd said was the result of reaching a stage in my counselling. After almost two years of help and support, I was growing stronger. I felt no need to be the kind of emotional punching bag I'd spent much of my life being.

It was a prescient moment, because only a few days later, while I was sitting on Town Hall station waiting for a connecting train to go to Adam's place for a party in the afternoon, Claudia rang again.

I was pleased to chat, although she sounded very low. She struggled to get the words out, but managed to say that she'd sent me an email, and was calling to check if I'd gotten it.

I hadn't, and said that I wouldn't be home for hours since the party was planned to run late. Something inspired me to make Claudia an offer in that moment. I asked her if she'd like me to delete the email, and I promised, as her friend, that I would honour my word and scrap it without reading one word.

'No,' Claudia struggled, 'I'd like you to read it,' she said.

I rolled my eyes, rang off, and promptly forgot all about it when joining the gathering on Tamarama Beach, which turned into a late lunch and dinner at Adam's place.

I'd never really enjoyed myself solely in the company of gay men, but on that day I let myself go a little and got past all the sexual politics by just surrendering to them. Some of the men were the kind who'd announce their perving proclivities out very loud so even their often unwilling subjects can hear them. That made me laugh.

Another, who held court in the kitchen, was a small, Buddha-like man who laughed so raucously you couldn't help but laugh with him.

He ran tantric sex courses and managed to string sex into every shred of conversation, all the while laughing his head off. I had never seen the likes.

I managed to chat a little with Adam, and he showed me his

music studio and his room at the top of the house. It was a beautiful space with views over the sea, and it felt very creative, but Adam was pained by his tantric-sex friend, still chortling downstairs, and asked me what we had spoken about.

I laughed because we'd all been simulating being ravished against the oven, and explained that Lisa was taking photographs while we all took turns. Adam was not impressed and seemed very upset with me, with his friend, and with everyone. I left not long afterwards, as confused as always about him.

When I got home, I opened Claudia's email. In it, she had terminated our friendship.

After eight years of being the closest of friends, through the best and worst life had to offer both of us; after picking her up and forgiving everything when she fell off the wagon; defending her actions against everyone in her family and all our friends, and helping her through the birth of her child, she said she felt it was okay to not be friends now.

I was not surprised.

I'd felt the hurt of this friendship ever since Claudia has ostracised me from her home in the weeks after Jono's death, although I thought we'd worked things out. I thought the forgiveness I'd shown Claudia amounted to something.

She was in very careless territory. I felt the weight of her addict's expectation of me as her loyal sounding board. If this was how it was going to end, this had never been friendship, it was something altogether more calculated.

I only needed to write one thing in my response: that Claudia was just adding herself to the very long line of people who were trying to tell me what the state of my world was. I would shrug her attempt off in the same way I had shrugged them all off, through a simple process of non co-operation.

She must have been waiting, because minutes later, Claudia rang. For a moment I believed that might mean our friendship was going to get a reprieve.

'You're very good with words,' she told me with a low, emotionless voice.

'I think we both are,' I replied, and started yet another grieving process.

LISA was keen to get out of the city for the Anzac Day long weekend, so we took the dogs and went to Kiama for the day and spent most of the afternoon in the sun of the headland, the wild ocean below sending waves up through the famous blowhole which turned water into air and sent it down as mist.

The dogs had an absolute ball frolicking across the grass, free of the confines of their courtyard. We trawled through the local op shops and tried to find a trace of Kiama's most famous son, the great Hollywood costume designer and winner of three Academy Awards, Orry-Kelly.

But there was not a plaque, not a statue, nothing.

Three Oscars. At that time, Australia's record-holder, who'd designed the fringed black dress made famous by Marilyn Monroe and her ukelele on the train in *Some Like it Hot*. Was none of that enough for the small coastal town south of Sydney to remember Orry-Kelly?

Part of me couldn't help but put this down to homophobia. Perhaps Orry got his ticket out of Kiama and had never looked back?

As the day waned, Lisa didn't seem keen to leave, and said she needed to feel the sand between her toes one more time before we drove home, then promptly disappeared into the toilet block. I didn't think anything of it until we got back to Pyrmont where she said she needed a pizza, which we had to wait for at the local takeaway.

Slightly annoyed, I arrived home and was in the middle of wondering why there was a light on, when a group of people shouted 'Happy Birthday' at me from behind various bits of furniture.

For a moment I thought I'd been broken into, but the faces became familiar in the half light — Jen, Annie, Naumi, Sarah, Tim, Adam, Gabriella, Dan, Antonio, Tamara, Sal and a few other new friends, a spread of food and lots to drink.

In the surprise, Olive got locked outside and was running up and down yipping to be let in, but when she came into her home, wide-eyed with the shock, she saw and smelled her friends, and her response was the night's highlight for me.

She spent the next few hours walking through the gathering catching up with the genuinely caring people in our lives, every bit as much as I did. If I'd had a tail, I would have been wagging it too.

The next day I went through my post and found a present from my brother. A book. The message in his card was a heartfelt wish that I read it and come to terms with it. The subject was a detailed guide for homosexual men about how misguided our desires were and how we could change them through Christianity.

I laughed it off, and before I could take in any more of its contents, Jen had torn the book apart and thrown the shreds in the bin.

AS the second anniversary of Jono's death loomed, great shifts in my life were still settling.

I'd lost another friend. I'd started a new job and saw less of my new friends from the recital hall. Annie went overseas on tour and Jen was preparing to leave for a six-month course in Stockholm.

At work, I pretended to not notice that a very important shoot was scheduled by one of our clients in the country town of Yass on the very day of Jono's anniversary.

I sat on the information for a little while, just in case the date changed and I'd made a fuss over nothing, but it did not budge. I decided to try pushing the emotions down and just go ahead with flying inland, producing, directing and flying back, all in the same day.

I didn't talk to anyone about it. In a sense I was testing myself to see if I could handle the inevitable 'life goes on' principle and just go through with it all, but as the day came close, I crumbled.

I couldn't face anyone. Here I was, in a position for which I'd had to demonstrate an ability to work under pressure, trapped in a bind which could see things go awry.

I wrote an email to the boss, Darryl, asking that I be allowed to stay at home that day, explaining succinctly why. The next morning, he asked if I'd like him to go in my place.

It was a relief, and he was a very good sport about it, laughing that he liked the odd chance to be back out in the field again. I wrote to the marketing rep who was co-ordinating the client and explained. She made it happen without me, and without fuss.

That day, I simply hunkered down at home with the dogs and videos, and let the world go on without me. Jen called in the afternoon to check on me. That's all I needed.

PERHAPS it was because of the end of my friendship with Claudia, but I didn't feel like visiting the Blue Mountains as often as I used.

I looked for excuses to not go up there anymore, and one of those was finding another counsellor in the city.

If full-time work was still going to be affected by my grief, I felt I'd better keep the counselling up, and find someone to see in the city.

So I took myself up to the sexual health clinic at Royal North Shore Hospital, a five-minute walk from work, and met David, a counsellor who was very keen to take me on, since it seemed they were not a particularly well-patronised clinic despite having the full range of services.

I got David up to speed on my story, and mentioned my inability to work on the second anniversary of Jono's death. He listened intently and seemed to understand the journey I had been on, although none of it surprised him much.

It became a crutch that I made more comfortable with padding, my new counselling. Michael, my counsellor in the Blue Mountains, was not in the least surprised by my change, and wished me all the best.

I got used to another man listening to me once every couple of weeks, at a crucial time when close ones needed to spread their wings in directions other than my grief.

ONE night after work, Adam called. He was in my area, could he come over? I said that would be fine, and within minutes he found his way to my door.

He declined my offer of going out for a drink, slumped himself down on my Seventies sofa and told me he'd been on a hook up with someone he'd met on the internet, someone who lived near me, and it had not gone well.

I didn't ask and he did not elaborate, but there was something not yet satiated about Adam that night. He'd come to see if whatever spark we'd had was alive, but it had died in me long before.

Not long after it became apparent we were not going to have sex, Adam was gone.

Turning down an offer of sex was something I'd taken a long time to come to terms with before Jono and I had met. When I came out, I was prone to all kinds of offers from all kinds of men, and more often than not, like a teenager on the town, I went with them.

But it was rarely satisfying for me or, I imagine, for them. Somehow my exterior never matched my interior.

I was giving out mixed messages about what I was capable of

emotionally and sexually, and there's nothing worse than sending mixed messages in the gay community, it can get you into all sorts of strife.

Adam's fleeting visit reminded me of the feeling of depression that came with my determination to not sleep with a man just because he was interested in me.

Years before, one man had crossed the country to offer his love in my kitchen, minutes after his friends had left for the train, only for me to say no to him.

Not because he was unattractive, a little because he was almost a generation older than me, but definitely because what we'd be doing was simply playing. Playing around sex. There was not much more to it than that. We hardly knew one another, not the basis for a great relationship.

Also in my past was another man who told everyone we both knew that I was his for the taking, that he'd be making his move on me any day soon. By the time I realised, it was almost too late. I'd been set up for dinner at his house, with a lesbian couple who were planning to leave early, on purpose.

On the way from the train station, I thought about sleeping with this man. He was handsome, yes, older by a long shot, true, what could be the harm?

Well, the harm could be that I'd probably need to get out of it after a few months and I'd have to hurt someone in the process, and it was not worth destroying the friendship.

Another old flame leaped at his chance to take me home from the pub one night, ravish me for hours, before it became clear he was incapable of getting an erection. When I raised the issue on our bushwalk the next day, he blamed me for his inability, and told me without a tinge of irony that his erectile dysfunction was proof of the fact that my body did not want to be made love to. Balls.

Yet another man had played me easily at an HIV-AIDS fundraiser and I took him home, drunk more on the validation of his presence than any alcohol intake. He proceeded to keep me as his bit on the side for the next six months, dodging my questions about his life left and right.

I had never been told by another that they 'had to see a man about a dog,' but that guy was my last. I was awkward, more like an eighteen-year-old in my head than pushing thirty, living my youth when my youth had long disappeared. I carried on about same-sex equality and HIV-AIDS as though I was an expert.

Jono was the only man who'd managed to silence me, and through his courageous manner of getting me to lighten up, he'd won me, body and soul.

Back in the horror I had run from, 'on the market', incapable of even creating a profile on an internet dating site, I yearned for the love I had found and just as quickly lost.

EIGHTEEN

DAVID SUGGESTED TO me very early in my new counselling sessions that I make a submission to an inquiry about same-sex relationships that was starting in Sydney very soon.

I had never heard of the Human Rights and Equal Opportunities Commission (HREOC), which has since changed its name to the Human Rights Commission.

In truth, I was sick of telling my story, trying to put it all into context for people who were too afraid to talk about death, so I said I'd think about it.

But the next time I went back, David handed me the paperwork.

Under the umbrella of Same Sex: Same Entitlements, HREOC had created a platform to illustrate exactly how I'd been treated, not on an emotional level, but a financial one.

The process of creating an estate for a deceased person is, at its core, financial. A funeral contract, with the resultant death certificate, is a financial tool; and navigating the work-life balance whilst in grief at the loss of a partner is a financial tightrope.

The counsellor assigned to me at Royal Prince Alfred Hospital the evening Jono died had made a point of telling me that I would be able to claim support benefits from Australia's social security system, via Centrelink, for funerary costs and on-going support, but it became apparent very quickly he was wrong — that organisation made absolutely no acknowledgement of same-sex relationships at that time, and I could not access any form of widow's pension.

I was lucky, I got through by living well within my means, but should it have been that way?

A HREOC submission could not just be a rant, crying 'it wasn't fair!' and letting them sort out why. I knew how easy, cold and definite my disenfranchisement had been, but when I researched the legislation which was so lacking it had allowed Maureen and Warren to do whatever they wanted, I knew I had a unique story to tell.

My submission was succinct — a page of emotionless fact about Centrelink's discrimination, about holes in the legislation which governed funeral directors in the creation of death certificates, and the NSW Attorney-General's tardiness in upholding state laws that had been in place for same-sex de-facto spouses for seven years.

I sent it in, and forgot all about it.

THE public holidays loomed large for me, working full-time again, so I endeavoured to get away from the city as much as I could. The June long weekend for the Queen's Birthday came around, and that meant the Blackheath Dance would be on again.

Naumi was keen, as was Sarah, our gang of 'mums on the run' as I called them, escaping kids and partners for one night of dancing every year in the safe confines of a gay and lesbian disco in the usually freezing Blackheath night.

Winter had embedded itself on the upper mountains and we crowded around Naumi's welcoming fire, going over Blackheath Dances past — the year Sarah 'cut a rug' before she knew she was pregnant with her first baby, literally spiraling to the floor in a knockout dance move; the year a double drag act called FLABBA won the talent show; and now, part of our mythology, the year we went two weeks after Jono died.

I got in Naumi's car and headed for the Chinese restaurant to collect our takeaways. Night had fallen and in the unfamiliar car I didn't anticipate the scuttle of a ringtail possum as it desperately bolted across my headlights, but I felt the soft bump as I rolled over it.

I pulled over and went back. There, trying to drag itself along, the injured possum expired.

Struck in the darkness by a sudden sense of futility, I sobbed from the pit of my soul. I am just not in the killing game.

But this needless, mistaken death baffled me. Why had it run, the silly thing? Why had I not seen it sooner? Why could I not save it, in this frozen night, from the pain of its death at my hands?

I could face it no more, not in the build up to going out for the night, so I dragged some leaves from the ditch, placed the poor creature under them, apologised, and moved on.

Back at the house I told the girls over dinner, noticed Naumi wince when another friend wanted to dwell on the death of the little possum. She knew I'd had enough of death and was probably in the market for nothing but life.

We took silly photos, toyed with a crazy wig which someone was going to wear. I put it on and decided to leave it on although it made me look like Shaggy from *Scooby-Doo*, and we disappeared into the cold night for the higher-altitude town of Blackheath.

The Blackheath Dance never changes. Enough time had passed since the tragic night two years before when I couldn't be there but couldn't be anywhere else, and I let myself move in the crowd.

The night was still young. So was I, only just, and the music had not descended into the terrible long medleys of hits which we'd all need a few drinks inside us to endure.

Plus I had a wig on. It made me taller, and I was already tall enough. It also disguised me, since I had very little hair and clipped my scalp very short. Some faces looked into mine, seeking, wondering, *is that him?* Others took me as I was, something new, no longer the same, transformed.

I saw and was seen by men who had bedded me, and men who had wanted to. It was familiar and almost not worth the effort of noticing. I was just myself, but not.

One young thing was very flirty, getting close, making all the eye contact you'd need to make it go somewhere. Naumi clocked it, danced over to me and danced the wig off. I felt a rush of cold to my scalp, and the rush of air as the young thing noticed my true appearance and danced away.

Then I stopped dancing. I just stopped. I'd had my turn, I suppose, and it had been wonderful.

You were wonderful Jono, you were the one for me, and I was the one for you.

I was one of the lucky ones who'd found true love. It had gone, after vanishing one random autumn night, but at least it had been. I would just have to live on, knowing that I had loved and been loved in return, but no more of this dance.

I started to nudge my way through celebrating bodies, felt the water forming across the surface of my eyes, found a clearing and turned towards the direction of the stacked chairs, when a woman in the middle of a dance move grabbed my hands in hers and drew me right inside her energetic life beat.

I surrendered. I had nothing else to do, no other purpose in that moment. Had I reached the chairs I would probably have buried my broken soul into my jacket and escaped to the railway station.

Instead, pure expression enveloped me. She was gorgeous, this creature, voluptuous and sensuous. With her cute little painted moustache, she seemed called-upon to give my spirit some kind of revival, some resuscitation of my own, to beat back the shadow of death that was making its latest attempt at closing my heart.

I would come to know this woman and tell her about how she saved me that night, although she never acknowledged it was anything more or less that what was needed in the moment, as she twirled me around and released me through a gap in the crowd that saw me land at the same moment as another man was turning and making his own retreat towards the chairs.

His face was familiar. *Him? Yes, it is him.* We turned and walked in tandem to the back. Same height, almost the same age. He was usually here with his boyfriend, who'd no doubt make an appearance soon.

Friends in common welcomed us both and poured us drinks. I was thirsty and I downed my booze fast, then asked where his boyfriend Patrick was.

'Patrick?' he said, quizzically, that beautiful smile rising. 'It's James, and he's not here. He's on the river, celebrating his fortieth.'

Oh?

'How are you?' he asked. He'd known Jono, had employed him as a waiter in his restaurant when Jono first came to the mountains.

I said I was okay. 'It's been a bit hard,' I replied. The usual platitudes.

I had another drink as he talked with Beth, and then another man turned up. My familiar man talked with him, they appeared to be meeting here, tonight.

I went up to Beth and asked her to remind me of my familiar man's name. 'Richard,' she yelled into my ear over the music.

Of course, Richard.

He was being very attentive to his friend, and they drifted off to another table together. Through the booze and emotion, about ten minutes later I realised Richard had just told me he was single.

We'd met eight years before at Katoomba Hospital on World AIDS day 1998, both of us volunteering at a lunch to thank the staff who'd given such long-term care to HIV-AIDS patients since the days when dying men had nowhere else to go.

On that day, Richard had been in charge of the barbecue, and when we were introduced I took in his large, handsome demeanour with a sudden rush to the head, but the man who introduced us made very sure I also knew Richard was spoken for.

I wasn't out, half an eye aware of running into one of Mum's nursing colleagues and finding myself having to explain why I was there.

All the lovely ones are married or straight, I thought, the joke only half working on my lonely soul.

But Richard remained on the edge of my life for years. We would see one another at parties, at the Blackheath Dance, and around the traps.

Jono and I met and started our relationship. He and I were

always slightly scared to socialise in the local gay community. We once waited in the car outside Richard and James' house trying to pluck up the courage to drop in one afternoon, then chickened out.

The rest of the latest dance went like a blur. Richard was there with that other man. They'd connected on the internet and this was their first meeting.

There was no spark between them that I could detect, although Richard was being a gentleman.

The talent show came and went, just like the night came and went, and the time arrived for the dance committee to turn on the lights, creating the last chance for company that night.

The mums were already on the move. Richard was standing across the hall. I decided that I had one chance to make a connection, get a number, anything.

So I paused. Just at that moment Richard's gaze met mine. It was one of those moments, across a smoky room — his eyes locked onto mine and I have been willingly under their gaze for the many years since.

I walked across to him and spoke the bravest direct words of my entire life.

THE morning of my submission to The Human Rights and Equal Opportunities Commission was one of those longed-for Blue Mountains winter days, with the bleakness chased away by a strong blast of sun. The weather might turn, but nothing beats those brilliant sunny mornings with bright light between the bare branches of European trees.

I'd asked for the morning off work to make my appearance at the hearing, and told the boss exactly why I wouldn't be there. Darryl nodded with approval, the kind that tells you times are changing fast in the Australian community.

I'd stayed at Richard's place the night before, a typical Katoomba weatherboard cottage around the corner from The Three Sisters, where we'd recently started our relationship.

Standing on the railway platform, watching the frozen branches thawing, I sensed how extremely lucky I was, because I wasn't forced to start this new adventure with a ghost between us, because Richard had also known Jono.

Jono had been a terrible waiter who made dreadful coffee. Richard recalled the day he was choreographing something by the waiters' station, attempting to explain himself in his usual whimsical way. It had made Richard laugh.

For years I would explain Jono's place in my life by introducing him to the conversation as 'my partner Jono, who died,' to give him his rightful place. Somehow, 'My ex, Jono,' never fit the bill.

Jono and I did not part in enmity, far from it, but we parted, nevertheless.

'Big smile,' Richard encouraged, when I explained I would have to attend a photo session after the hearing for the Fairfax journalist who was writing about those giving live submissions to HREOC.

IN the hearing rooms, the HREOC staff reminded me the media would be there at the end of the morning sessions, but right then the room was reverent. People gathered in whispered tones, before the Human Rights Commissioner of the day — Graeme Innes — entered and we got underway.

As I listened to each submission, I had a creeping sense of irrelevance. Now, I put this down to denial, the remnant emotions that even then, more than two years after Jono's death, tried to convince me that none of it had happened, or that it was someone else's life which was being presented to the room.

Other same-sex attracted people explained the various ways we were all being excluded from life's processes on a financial level.

One of the most compelling was the story of an older widow who'd had a very long relationship with a war veteran and been totally excluded in his partner's estate and denied a sizeable veteran's pension.

With that story ringing in my ears I went up to the table and started my submission. By then, I was so full of emotion it spilled out into the microphone with plosive discord, and someone crouched in front of the table to adjust the mic's position a little further away.

I explained that I wished I had bought a photograph of Jono with me. I knew the very one.

It was a selfie we'd taken at the end of a photo shoot in front of an abandoned building at the top of the Katoomba street we lived on, when we'd been creating black and white professional headshots for one another.

Jono worked the camera to his best advantage, his modelling skill kicking in, and nearly every shot was perfect. He encouraged me to relax and pose this way and that, but there was barely a decent shot amongst mine.

When the headshots were done, we took some of ourselves together, resulting in a series of images with our heads pressed together in a way that makes us look like one being. Natural, broad smiles, nothing to express or sell, just us.

The last of those shots was the one I imagined in the hearing.

In it, Jono — my lost boy — appeared in very soft focus, disappearing from the lens, his head tucked into my jaw as though seeking protection. In the light of his untimely death, it's something of a frightening image, but as the photograph of two men who were everything to one another, it hid nothing.

However, at the hearing it was just me and the room, and I struggled to keep back the tears. When this happens to me I tip into anger.

Tears, or anger, these are my only options when forced to speak the awful truth. For me, anger gets more out.

I made my points, but I went the extra mile, and explained how all this disenfranchisement could be ameliorated by legislation, that the easiest way to protect same-sex attracted people in relationships was to allow us a non-onerous form of coupling under the law.

That was 2006, a time when such a thing seemed like a very big ask indeed.

My job done, one of the HREOC staff ushered me out of the room, where the media I'd forgotten about confronted me.

Radio journalists, mainly, were rushing to get the story onto the midday news. I don't recall what I said, but a friend said my voice surprised him by making a relevant dent in the ABC regular lunchtime current affairs program.

Adele Horin, at that time one of Fairfax's stable of excellent journalists, said she would contact me by phone for more detail later.

She rang while I was at work that afternoon, issues of video production absorbing my mind. She was attempting, as all good journalists do, to understand my story in a way which would fit into her article but could take a unique place of its own, yet across the course of our conversation she kept hitting the same stumbling block: the reasons why Jono's relatives did what they did.

To understand my story, Adele would need to find a way of acknowledging that a mother and brother had made such effective attempts to tread on the human rights of their son and brother's long-term partner.

So my burgeoning journalistic streak kicked in, and I suggested to Adele that she contact Maureen and Warren directly if she needed clarification on any of the details I'd given and the claims I'd made.

She understood my point without me having to explain — I was offering a right of reply about everything I'd said.

The article was not due to be published for a few days in the weekend edition of *The Sydney Morning Herald*. Maureen and Warren could easily have been contacted for comment by phone.

Something about my willingness to have my story checked by its villains meant more to Adele than any difficulty she had getting her head around the aberration, and she went to print with my account — that my name had been kept from Jono's death certificate wilfully and in breach of the law.

All of us who'd been at the HREOC hearing were called to the Fairfax offices in south Sydney later that day for the photo shoot.

We were lined up in front of a white cyclorama for an image the photographer revealed would emulate those group *Vanity Fair*-type group shots.

But he didn't have the luxury of image manipulation — he needed to capture a group of undistinguished gay and lesbian people without technology or enhancement, without hairdressing and make up or fancy lighting. We would be revolutionary, indeed.

Big smile, I recalled as the flashes went off.

Big smiles from the disenfranchised.

Big smile from the lucky, lucky man who'd found enduring love twice in one lifetime, and would go on to make a family again.

NINETEEN

THE shock of Jono's death lasted for a few years. Richard learned to recognise the differences in my behaviour, what was grief and what was not. It was painful territory to traverse, especially since these years were lived in the Blue Mountains, where Richard and I bought a house and renovated an old garden.

Sometimes I'd find myself seeking out the haunts of my years with Jono. One night I went to the service station for milk with my oldest dog in the car, and we stopped outside the house Jono and I shared. Olive squealed with delight as we approached the gate, the lights from inside the weatherboard cottage burning brightly, and she couldn't understand why we were not opening the gate and entering the house again, back into our old life.

Near Jono's little cottage opposite the technical college there was unlimited parking all day. Many times I'd leave the car there and find myself overwhelmed by thoughts of my lost boy and the courageous new start he'd made in that house after moving from Bellingen, and from where his life had grown, with me at his side.

The traces of him have faded over the years since his death. Olive responded to hearing his name for the rest of her long life, and Tully continues to, but it is with a sense of resignation, not their former ardent hope that he is about to appear.

I have fought with the fear of losing another husband, and still struggle with the emotions if it's already dark of an evening and I am not sure where Richard is, and the phone rings, and I don't answer it.

What new life might I find waiting for me when I play the message?

Because we started our relationship in our very late thirties, the first flush of youth was long behind us, and we both had baggage.

Richard is a stage-four melanoma survivor of fifteen years, so there are health issues I could dwell on, but I push those aside with a thought for the circumstances of Jono's death — the youngish man who died seemingly for no reason — and I take courage.

Richard's family has had to face the politics of LGBTIQA+ equality as a necessary add-on to my presence in their lives, and they have done this with courage.

We have lived together, barely spent a night apart, married in a civil union in New Zealand, renovated, gardened, lived, loved, fought, made up and been the best partners we can be, Richard and I, and Jono has been there in his own small way.

Yet he dwindles. Only this year I realised that something I often say to Richard is the same gentle, funny, showbiz comment Jono and I would regularly say to one another, only it leaves Richard feeling the opposite of the intended support, so Jono's got to diminish just that little bit more.

It's right, and it's no one's fault, but it still hurts.

And the plans we made with one another, the ones that I have tried to bring to life without him, they also have been in vain. It is truly a different world, this world without Jono.

IN May 2007, Human Rights Commissioner Graeme Innes presented the *Same Sex: Same Entitlements* report to federal Attorney-

General Phillip Ruddock, the same man who had so enthusiastically quashed the chances of marriage equality in Australia three years prior.

The report identified almost seventy pieces of Commonwealth legislation in which same-sex attracted Australians were financially disenfranchised.

Mr Ruddock and Prime Minister John Howard sat on the report, but opposition leader for the Australian Labor Party, Kevin Rudd, turned its implementation into an immediate election promise. Just months later, he swept eleven years of conservative Liberal government from office.

After forming his cabinet, Kevin Rudd ensured the recommendations of *Same Sex: Same Entitlements* were adopted, which resulted in an audit revealing there were actually more like one-hundred pieces of legislation that treated same-sex attracted Australians differently in an economic sense.

By 2009, all such laws were amended, but marriage equality got lost in the revolving door of leadership.

While he held the majority of seats in Australia's House of Representatives, Kevin Rudd — a Christian — stopped short of leading his party to any kind of legislation allowing same-sex unions to be solemnised.

Marriage equality advocates therefore watched with great interest in 2010 when Julia Gillard took over the job of Australia's Prime Minister.

An avowed atheist in a de-facto relationship, she presented as a leader who understood the need for choice where relationships were concerned, but she publicly stated her opposition to marriage equality ahead of the 2010 federal election.

At the Labor Party's 2011 national conference, when the party endorsed a platform in support of marriage equality, Julia Gillard sponsored another motion that was immediately passed, granting a free vote to all Labor ministers.

Subsequently, she led many of her Labor colleagues across the floor to sit alongside Tony Abbott and the conservative Liberal opposition to resoundingly vote down marriage equality in 2012.

For many Australians, it was an incongruous — and unforgettable — alliance.

Before his second incarnation as Prime Minister in 2013, and after the publication of a searing essay about his 'road to Damascus' moment on the issue, Kevin Rudd became Australia's highest-profile Christian and politician ever to support marriage equality.

His reason: he understood there was 'angst' in the community about marriage equality. At that point, I started to pay attention to the debate again. Angst was the perfect word to describe what I had endured.

Community support for marriage equality, which once languished in the thirtieth percentile under John Howard in the year Jono died, sat at around 70 per cent support during the 2013 federal election campaign.

But when Tony Abbott reclaimed the government for the Liberal Party, it was without a single promise on relationship legislation for same-sex couples, just a vague indication that the Coalition party room would get the chance to debate marriage equality if a Bill ever came before parliament.

A MONTH after the election Julia Gillard never got to contest because her own party backed Kevin Rudd over her, she was welcomed to the stage at the Sydney Opera House by a wall of applause for a live interview with writer and broadcaster Anne Summers.

Twitter fired up in support of Australia's first female Prime Minister, and the sentiment was loud and clear: she had been robbed of the job, and we had been robbed of a great leader.

Some of us threw in a few reminders about her objectionable, inexplicable stance against marriage equality, which over the years had become a mantra bordering on a drone: *I believe marriage is between a man and a woman.*

During Summers' interview, Gillard was relaxed and worldly wise, speaking off the cuff, answering all manner of questions openly and honestly.

If there was a script, she was clearly off it, even when Summers went into very personal territory and raised the subject of a *Woman's Day* article that suggested Gillard and her de-facto partner Tim Mathieson were having relationship problems.

'I wasn't even asked,' Julia Gillard explained about the content of the article.

'Something we were never given a proper opportunity to comment on,' she added.

'Accuracy would be desirable.'

I recognised her words and sentiments from my experience of Jono's mother and brother, when their trash-talk and lies about my relationship were able to go unchallenged.

Then, just when it seemed as though the interview was wrapping up, the last question came from a young boy — Saxon — who asked Julia Gillard why she wouldn't allow LGBTIQA+ to marry.

The audience applauded explosively and listened.

Could an intelligent, erudite, well-respected leader, an experienced lawyer with a background in social justice, who'd been free to choose the form of relationship that suited her, really not understand the need for marriage equality?

Or were the rumours true — that Julia Gillard had agreed to halt the advance of marriage equality in exchange for support from one of Australia's largest and most conservative trade unions, backing which secured her position as Prime Minister?

As she answered young Saxon, Gillard's script started. Knowing that she would be asked about her great anomaly, she dodged the issue entirely with a prepared anti-marriage answer to a pro-equality question.

Some commentators congratulated her on what seemed like a feminist clarion call, but an anti-marriage stance is not a radical notion in a country which has enjoyed de-facto laws and fault-free divorce for over three decades.

As the gloss dried on her retrograde answer, I bid Julia Gillard farewell from the debate. One day, I felt sure, she'd be forced to explain herself.

When we at last have marriage equality in this country, after the damage they caused, many current and former politicians would be wise to avoid inviting themselves to the party.

Kevin Rudd's name will be on my list, however.

The motives behind his backflip on marriage equality were widely questioned or written off, but it's been largely forgotten he went to the 2013 federal election with a promise to bring a marriage equality bill before parliament within his first one-hundred days of government.

Anyone who thought he was not to be trusted on this issue forgot that Kevin Rudd was the only leader of this era with a record for delivering on a promise made to the LGBTIQA+ community during an election campaign.

ALMOST a decade since my last visit, I returned to Bellingen with Richard.

The township was bursting under the same pressures as always, a stunning environment in distress under the weight of visitor expectation.

Richard and I were no different, getting annoyed at not being able to find a car park, and at the terrible turn the weather had taken. Our lunch companion was on Bellingen time and very late.

Before we left town, I asked Richard to drive the familiar streets to see the large house Maureen had built by knocking Joe's down, the one with the great view from the mountains to the ocean.

I remembered the architect's plans, three storeys of harsh brown blocks, with gaping windows and wide decks, a swimming pool along one side, and a vast terrace off Maureen's bedroom from which she'd be able to see the ocean.

I knew Maureen still lived there, so we drove the way that would conceal the car from the house behind a stand of trees. As we crested the hill I craned my neck to take in the monstrosity.

But it was not there.

I was thrown, and while Richard struggled to turn the car on the slope, I saw the thick row of concrete footings where the architect-designed pool was supposed to be, covered in weeds; old weeds that had died and been covered by new weeds, season after season.

Some kind of development had been started, but it had been called to a halt, years ago. Joe's house was still intact, with its original blonde bricks, brown tiles and white handrails.

There was the window of the room Jono and I regularly shared.

There was the terrace Joe loved to sit on and talk about his view, although the place had a silent, lonely feeling.

We were gone before we were even there, and soon after we turned onto the road through the darkening valley towards the coast, I felt my well-loved heart opening to Maureen and Warren and all their failed dreams, and I knew I had truly survived.

Afterword

2015

ALTHOUGH THIS BOOK is about homophobia in a much broader sense than it is about marriage equality, it is impossible to put a full stop on *Questionable Deeds* without outlining the terrible holding pattern Australia is still experiencing on this human right during the month I committed this book to print.

Multiple marriage equality bills have been brought before Australia's parliament, but each has been evaded by the majority of our government ministers.

The issue has been a political football across two decades, booted between our House of Representatives, Senate and High Court.

Marriage equality legislation has been passed — and overturned — at state level, and the government is now proposing a plebiscite or referendum after the next election, while the opposition has pledged to bring yet another bill before parliament if it wins.

Meanwhile, our cultural and political allies — Canada, New Zealand, England, Ireland and the United States — have already passed marriage equality into law, as Australia's community support for it continues to climb to the highest percentage ever.

Since becoming a marriage equality advocate in the wake of Jono's death, I have witnessed plenty of reasons why people don't support marriage equality, and they're not all about homophobia.

Some of my biggest shocks about this came from within the LGBTIQA+ community, where there has long been significant resistance to marriage because it's seen as too heteronormative.

Many feminists disagree with marriage equality along the same lines as Julia Gillard's opposition to marriage as an outdated institution.

There are those who believe de-facto laws are enough for any two people in Australia to prove the existence of a legally recognised marriage-like relationship, without requiring the 'one piece of paper' that a marriage contract provides.

However, since the 2015 parliamentary winter break, what I have found most eye opening is the swift softening of many a hardline stance against equal marriage for LGBTIQA+.

In addition to the regular declarations of federal ministers of all stripes, changing their positions to one in support of marriage equality, many of the country's most outspoken opponents have followed suit.

I have no idea what to put these shifts down to.

I imagine some Australians are waking up to the way homophobia works in politics, where it's disguised behind a belligerent wall of dissembling.

I suspect many equality naysayers have come to terms with a great reality: that not everyone in the LGBTIQA+ community wants to emulate straight marriage, whatever 'straight marriage' is.

Surely there is also enough experience of LGBTIQA+ within the community by now that a stronger understanding of our equality has emerged.

Whatever the reasons, as more people change, it's possible that the 'equality' in marriage equality is what makes it challenging for the last sections of society that oppose it.

Jono and I maintained a very equal relationship. For me, equality is the only way to roll as one of a couple — replacing sublimation, name changing, dowries and obedience with negotiation, a right to speak, mutual support, give and take, and win-win, especially when it comes to conflict.

Living in an equal relationship means there's no one else to blame — not your religion, culture, gender, parents, family, orientation, government, other relationships or your politics.

Equal relationships are way more than a right, they're the ultimate in personal responsibility and, by extension, the highest responsibility between partners.

Same-sex attracted people have spent decades, if not centuries, working on relationships that function — often far more equally than our straight counterparts — outside the traditional legislative and religious paradigms of marriage.

It is time to have our experience rewarded by access to the full range of relationship choices.

But the fight for equality will not end with that. I have never believed marriage equality is the last step in fighting homophobia, heteronormative paradigms or misogyny.

It is the first step, and when it is achieved, we will have reached the time to begin changing the truly prejudiced hearts and minds.

We will have reached the time to debate relationship equality in a practical instead of a theoretical manner.

Although it will be a major challenge for many, we will have reached the time to consider inclusive sex education, in order that all children learn about sex long before they are left to the kind of desperate learning processes — often illegal — that so many are currently prone to at beats, saunas, and online.

And we will also have reached the time of no more excuses for any Attorney-General to operate outside the legislation of a secular society when managing the creation of official documents.

It will be a time when a death certificate can be created legally and accurately for an **LGBTIQA+** person who lived in any kind of relationship in this country, and their surviving spouse.

Equal births, deaths and marriages will be just the beginning.

2021

IN 2016, I joined the campaign to prevent a public vote on the human rights issue of marriage equality. We stopped Tony Abbott's plebiscite but lost the battle over his replacement Malcolm Turnbull's expensive, divisive survey, which took place in 2017.

The result was what campaigners had told politicians for a decade: the vast majority of Australians support marriage between any two people regardless of gender.

Subsequently, the Australian parliament passed marriage equality in December of that year.

Jono's mother didn't live long enough to see it.

The battle to keep **LGBTIQA+** safe at school continues.

After being together for twelve years, Richard and I were married under Australian law in May, 2018, but that's another story altogether...

Acknowledgements

A BOOK NEVER just happens all by itself, and this one was no different.

I am extremely grateful to have benefitted from two expert readers of my final drafts — writers Mary Moody and Sarah Michell — whose considered responses helped shape this book.

I also want to acknowledge my sister Jen, who helped put many events in their correct place and order where my grief had clouded an accurate memory; and because she always courageously reads her brother's work, no matter what she might discover about him!

I am indebted to Shelley Argent for writing the foreword (and updating it in 2021). I have long admired her activism on behalf of the same-sex attracted community and our families, and I acknowledge that PFLAG's work goes a very long way towards preventing the kind of situation I endured after Jono's death.

Journalist Margo Kingston has been a staunch supporter of my writing and it was a conversation with her that gave me the courage to embark on what I see as a long-form piece of journalism.

During the proofreading process, Elizabeth Ferretti was the cavalry responsible for the polish on this publication.

It was a hectic time during which I was also assisted with medical research by Dr Mary Russell, and last-minute design assistance from Steve Whitfield for the cover of the first edition.

This book was rejected by every publisher and agent I could get a manuscript to. This was often slow and painful, sometimes swift and hilarious, but never easy.

For that reason I also need to thank the many people who taught me the art of editing and publishing over the past twenty years — my expert colleagues and friends who freely shared their skills.

In this digital age of stripped-back, self-sufficient, online, independent publishing, those experiences served me well when navigating the pathway to publishing my work regardless. This ongoing process led to the creation of the High Country Books imprint.

Finally, heartfelt thanks to my husband Richard, who counselled, listened, championed and encouraged this publication out of me, and, with grace and irreplaceable generosity, never requires me to forget Jono.

High Country Books is an imprint of The Makers Shed
publishing a select range of fiction and non-fiction
www.themakersshed.org

*The High Country Books logo is based on a copper and sterling-silver brooch
created by Richard Moon Wearable Silver & Silverware. The design is derived from a
eucalyptus leaf, symbolising the well-forested mountains of Australia's high-altitude regions.*

www.ingramcontent.com/pod-product-compliance
Lightning Source LLC
Chambersburg PA
CBHW030253010526
44107CB00053B/1695